MILITARY ASSESSMENT OF RUSSIAN ACTIVITIES AND SECURITY CHALLENGES IN EUROPE

COMMITTEE ON ARMED SERVICES
HOUSE OF REPRESENTATIVES

ONE HUNDRED FIFTEENTH CONGRESS

FIRST SESSION

HEARING HELD
MARCH 28, 2017

U.S. GOVERNMENT PUBLISHING OFFICE

25–091   WASHINGTON : 2017

For sale by the Superintendent of Documents, U.S. Government Publishing Office
Internet: bookstore.gpo.gov   Phone: toll free (866) 512–1800; DC area (202) 512–1800
Fax: (202) 512–2104   Mail: Stop IDCC, Washington, DC 20402–0001

COMMITTEE ON ARMED SERVICES

One Hundred Fifteenth Congress

WILLIAM M. "MAC" THORNBERRY, Texas, *Chairman*

WALTER B. JONES, North Carolina
JOE WILSON, South Carolina
FRANK A. LoBIONDO, New Jersey
ROB BISHOP, Utah
MICHAEL R. TURNER, Ohio
MIKE ROGERS, Alabama
TRENT FRANKS, Arizona
BILL SHUSTER, Pennsylvania
K. MICHAEL CONAWAY, Texas
DOUG LAMBORN, Colorado
ROBERT J. WITTMAN, Virginia
DUNCAN HUNTER, California
MIKE COFFMAN, Colorado
VICKY HARTZLER, Missouri
AUSTIN SCOTT, Georgia
MO BROOKS, Alabama
PAUL COOK, California
JIM BRIDENSTINE, Oklahoma
BRAD R. WENSTRUP, Ohio
BRADLEY BYRNE, Alabama
SAM GRAVES, Missouri
ELISE M. STEFANIK, New York
MARTHA McSALLY, Arizona
STEPHEN KNIGHT, California
STEVE RUSSELL, Oklahoma
SCOTT DesJARLAIS, Tennessee
RALPH LEE ABRAHAM, Louisiana
TRENT KELLY, Mississippi
MIKE GALLAGHER, Wisconsin
MATT GAETZ, Florida
DON BACON, Nebraska
JIM BANKS, Indiana
LIZ CHENEY, Wyoming

ADAM SMITH, Washington
ROBERT A. BRADY, Pennsylvania
SUSAN A. DAVIS, California
JAMES R. LANGEVIN, Rhode Island
RICK LARSEN, Washington
JIM COOPER, Tennessee
MADELEINE Z. BORDALLO, Guam
JOE COURTNEY, Connecticut
NIKI TSONGAS, Massachusetts
JOHN GARAMENDI, California
JACKIE SPEIER, California
MARC A. VEASEY, Texas
TULSI GABBARD, Hawaii
BETO O'ROURKE, Texas
DONALD NORCROSS, New Jersey
RUBEN GALLEGO, Arizona
SETH MOULTON, Massachusetts
COLLEEN HANABUSA, Hawaii
CAROL SHEA–PORTER, New Hampshire
JACKY ROSEN, Nevada
A. DONALD McEACHIN, Virginia
SALUD O. CARBAJAL, California
ANTHONY G. BROWN, Maryland
STEPHANIE N. MURPHY, Florida
RO KHANNA, California
TOM O'HALLERAN, Arizona
THOMAS R. SUOZZI, New York
(Vacancy)

Robert L. Simmons II, *Staff Director*
Catherine Sendak, *Professional Staff Member*
Katy Quinn, *Professional Staff Member*
Britton Burkett, *Clerk*

CONTENTS

MILITARY ASSESSMENT OF RUSSIAN ACTIVITIES AND SECURITY CHALLENGES IN EUROPE

————————

HOUSE OF REPRESENTATIVES,
COMMITTEE ON ARMED SERVICES,
Washington, DC, Tuesday, March 28, 2017.

The committee met, pursuant to call, at 10:02 a.m., in room 2118, Rayburn House Office Building, Hon. William M. "Mac" Thornberry (chairman of the committee) presiding.

OPENING STATEMENT OF HON. WILLIAM M. "MAC" THORNBERRY, A REPRESENTATIVE FROM TEXAS, CHAIRMAN, COMMITTEE ON ARMED SERVICES

The CHAIRMAN. Committee will come to order.

Last week the committee heard from experts on hybrid warfare, which is also known by several other names. Today we focus on one of the regions that has experienced many, if not most, of the tactics that we had discussed.

From the little green men in Ukraine, to political assassinations as recently as last week, to buying influence in political parties, snap exercises to intimidate neighbors, and, of course, cyberattacks of various kinds, Europe has seen all of that and more.

Meanwhile, the Russians continue to invest in their nuclear weapons, their anti-access/area-denial capability, and in a variety of other capabilities designed to reduce or eliminate any technological military advantage that the United States may have had in the past. We know that one of their primary goals is to divide and weaken NATO [North Atlantic Treaty Organization], arguably the most successful military alliance ever.

To discuss these issues today we are pleased to welcome NATO Supreme Allied Commander and commander of the U.S. European Command, General Curtis Scaparrotti, not for the first time, but for the first time in this capacity.

Before turning to him, let me yield to Mr. Smith for any comments he would like to make.

STATEMENT OF HON. ADAM SMITH, A REPRESENTATIVE FROM WASHINGTON, RANKING MEMBER, COMMITTEE ON ARMED SERVICES

Mr. SMITH. Thank you, Mr. Chairman.

And welcome, General. It is great to see you again. I always appreciated your leadership out at Joint Base Lewis-McChord when you were out there and appreciate your leadership even more in Europe.

And I agree with the chairman's opening remarks, look forward to your testimony.

But Europe is, you know, as great a challenge as we have had since the end of the Cold War now. And I won't belabor the point because we have all heard about it, but Russia is reasserting itself not just in Eastern Europe but in many ways in Western Europe, trying to influence elections, trying—basically trying to undermine liberal democracy.

Vladimir Putin's goal is to make the world safe for autocratic dictatorships and to undermine the values that we hold dear in this country, which is representative democracy. And he is doing that, frankly, on a very low budget using a lot of cyber and a lot of intel operations, and I think we have to get smarter about how we counter that. And a lot has been said about that. I look forward to your comments.

Last thing I will say is, obviously the big question we have is what should our presence be in Europe as a deterrent to what Russia is doing? Because that, I think, should be the goal.

Putin is not stupid. They are nowhere near as strong as they were during the height of the Cold War. So basically he is trying to have influence on the cheap, but the higher the cost the less likely he is to engage in his destabilization efforts.

Does a larger presence by us in that region act as that deterrent? And if so, what should that presence look like?

So those are some of the questions I know we need answered. And obviously, you know, we want to reaffirm our commitment to NATO and its enduring importance in all of our alliances in Europe in terms of maintaining the peace and stability in the world that we want.

With that, I yield back. I look forward to your testimony.

The CHAIRMAN. General, without objection your full written statement will be made part of the record, and at this time you are recognized for any comments you would like to make. Thanks again for being here.

STATEMENT OF GEN CURTIS M. SCAPARROTTI, USA, COMMANDER, UNITED STATES EUROPEAN COMMAND

General SCAPARROTTI. Well, thank you.

Chairman Thornberry and Ranking Member Smith and distinguished members of the committee, I am honored to testify today as the commander of the United States European Command. On behalf of over 60,000 permanently signed service members as well as civilians, contractors, and their families who serve and represent our Nation in Europe, thank you for your support.

European theater remains critical to our national interest. The transatlantic alliance gives us a unique advantage over our adversaries: a united, capable warfighting alliance resolved in its purpose and strengthened by shared values that have been forged in battle.

EUCOM's [U.S. European Command's] relationship with NATO and the 51 countries within our AOR [area of responsibility] provides the United States with a network of willing partners who support global operations and secure the international rules-based order. Our security architecture provides more than 1 billion people a safeguarded transatlantic trade, which now constitutes almost half of the world's GDP [gross domestic product].

However, this security architecture is being tested, and today we face the most dynamic European strategic environment in recent history. Political volatility and economic uncertainty are compounded by threats to our security system that are transregional, multi-domain, and multifunctional.

In the east, a resurgent Russia has turned from partner to antagonist as it seeks to reemerge as a global power. Countries along Russia's periphery, including Ukraine and Georgia, struggle against Moscow's malign activities and military actions.

In the southeast, strategic drivers of instability converge on key allies—especially Turkey, which has to simultaneously manage Russia, terrorists, and refugee flows.

In the south, violent extremists and transnational criminal elements spawn terror and corruption from North Africa to the Middle East, while refugees flee to Europe in search of security and opportunity.

And in the high north, Russia is reasserting its military presence and positioning itself for strategic advantage in the Arctic.

In response to these challenges, EUCOM has shifted its focus from security cooperation and engagement to deterrence and defense. Accordingly, we are adjusting our posture, plans, and readiness so that we remain relevant to the threats we face. In short, we are returning to our historic role as a warfighting command focused on deterrence and defense.

EUCOM's transition would not be possible without congressional support of the European Reassurance Initiative. Thanks in large measure to ERI, over the last 12 months EUCOM has made clear progress with an enhanced force presence, complex exercises and training, infrastructure improvements, increased pre-positioning of equipment and supplies, and partner capacity-building throughout Europe.

But we cannot meet these challenges alone. In response to Russian aggression EUCOM has continued to strengthen our relationship with strategic allies and partners, including the Baltic nations, Poland, Turkey, and Ukraine. EUCOM has also strengthened ties with Israel, one of our closest allies.

Above all, EUCOM has supported the NATO alliance, which remains, as Secretary Mattis said, "the bedrock for our transatlantic security."

Thus, the EUCOM posture is growing stronger, and I remain confident in our ability to affect this transition. But there is much work to do.

We must not only match but outpace the modernization advances of our adversaries. We must invest in the tools and capabilities needed to increase effectiveness across the spectrum of conflict. And we must ensure that we have a force that is credible, agile, and relevant to the dynamic demands of this theater.

To this end, EUCOM has identified the following focus areas: ISR [intelligence, surveillance, and reconnaissance] collection platforms to improve timely threat information and strategic warning; land force capabilities to deter Russia from further aggression; enhanced naval capabilities for antisubmarine warfare, strike warfare, and amphibious operations; pre-positioned equipment to increase our responsiveness to crisis; and enhanced missile defense systems.

Let me conclude by again thanking this committee's members and staff for their continued support of EUCOM, not only through increased funding, but also by helping us articulate the challenges that lie before us. Support from the other leaders and, above all, from the public at home and across Europe is vital [to] ensuring that we have a ready and a relevant force.

This remains a pivotal time for EUCOM as we transition to meet the demands of a dynamic security environment, and I remain confident that through the strength of our alliances and partnerships, and with the professionalism of our service members, we will adapt and ensure that Europe remains whole, free, and at peace.

Thank you.

And, Chairman, I look forward to the questions.

[The prepared statement of General Scaparrotti can be found in the Appendix on page 43.]

The CHAIRMAN. Thank you, sir.

Both Mr. Smith and I mentioned some of the tactics Russia has used, but can you step back for a second and summarize in, obviously, this open session what they are doing with their military capability? How and in what areas are they advancing their capability, and how does it relate to us? Just kind of a general picture of their military capabilities.

General SCAPARROTTI. Chairman, thank you.

I think if you look at their forces from what we know as hybrid or asymmetric means, to conventional, to nuclear, they are modernizing this force in every one of those categories. Within the hybrid, for instance, we are well aware of their use of cyber, their use of disinformation, or "information confrontation," as they call it. And, in fact, in recent months they announced new elements within their force that focus on information confrontation, information operations.

So they are focused on that and, in fact, I would add here that when you look at their view of the spectrum of conflict, unlike our view, theirs includes those activities below what we would call the level of, or the threshold of, conflict. It includes political provocation, information operations, disinformation, cyber, et cetera. So it is a functional part now of their doctrine, I believe, and they put it into play.

In the conventional realm they are upgrading the systems that they have—their naval ships, their airplanes, et cetera—as well as building new ones for the future. They have refitted their aircraft and their ships for some of their newer munitions, which are very capable.

Caliber [cruise missile] system, for instance, can be placed on the ground, in the air, at sea, so it is a multifunctional system, gives them, you know, long reach and precision, et cetera. So that is how they are advancing in their force.

Their nuclear forces, as well. Across all the areas they have been increasing their capability, really refining their capability from the old systems.

And one of the things you see that is disturbing is the fact that they are using similar weapon systems that can either be conventional or nuclear, which then makes it difficult for us to clearly understand what they have employed. And then secondly, within their doctrine again, they have made the statement openly that they see a use for nuclear tactical capabilities within what we would consider a conventional conflict, which is very alarming.

So that is how I would—I would categorize their movement at this time.

The CHAIRMAN. Okay.

Let me just remind all members that immediately following this open hearing we will have a closed session with General Scaparrotti where we can go into more detail on classified matters. Again, that will be immediately upon the conclusion of this open hearing.

Mr. Smith.

Mr. SMITH. Thank you, Mr. Chairman.

Could you give us some idea of the importance of the presence of U.S. troops in Europe as a deterrent to what Russia is doing? And what size force do we have there now? What size force do you think we should have? And how would that presence help us to deter the activity that has been described?

General SCAPARROTTI. Well, first of all our presence there is and always has been a very important component of the alliance, the NATO—you know, NATO alliance, of which we are one of 28 nations, as well as our partners in Europe.

We have the best military in the world. It works across multi-domain, it is a joint functional force, and it provides a critical element to our partners. It also, in operating with them, builds interoperability which is essential, you know, within the alliance itself.

Today we have about a little over **60,000** of all services stationed in Europe. It provides a force that allows us to deter today but, as you know, with this committee and ERI we are looking to modernize that force to put us in a better posture, particularly given Russia's modernization that they are on that I just described.

We need a greater force there, I think, potentially in the land component, either a rotational or rotational enduring footprint of an armored division, for instance.

Within the Air Force we have a pretty good posture there, a very capable posture. But again, they are looking forward to adding, you know, fifth-generation aircraft, which are important given the modernization, again, of Russia.

And with the Navy, again, an additional naval component on rotation through Europe in order to deter, but specifically with respect to antisubmarine warfare, which is an area of concern with the Russians. We are still dominant in that domain, but we have to continue to invest in order to properly deter and also remain dominant.

Mr. SMITH. Thank you. One last question: Specifically on the Ukraine, what more could we be doing to help the Ukraine both fight off the Russian insurgency in the East and then also to strengthen their government, which I understand is, you know, plagued by corruption and plagued by inefficiency and that is part of the problem?

Because if Putin is unsuccessful in the Ukraine or if the cost gets too high for his interference there I think that is, you know, the best deterrent we could give to further activity because that is sort of, you know, where—I don't know if it is where he started, but it is certainly where he has had the most public involvement. What more could we be doing in the Ukraine?

General SCAPARROTTI. Sir, I have been to Ukraine twice now, both in their training area and out to the ATO [anti-terrorist operation zone]. I would say first of all I am very impressed with their military and its discipline. What we have provided them in terms of our training capability as well as equipment is being well used, and they are very eager in terms of their ability to learn more.

So we presently are involved in reform of their government and capacity-building within their security system. We need to continue that.

I don't know that it is more; I think it is probably a little better organization across the whole of government. Within the training environment, what we do with other NATO allies there is very effective.

Again, there, I have been out to it and seen it done over the past year. I think better organization there would help. There are things we can do to continue to refine it.

The Ukrainian forces are learning and they are getting better, and we need to consistently adjust.

In terms of weaponry, I personally believe that we need to consider lethal defensive weapons for Ukraine. They are fighting a very lethal, tough enemy.

It is a Russian proxy, really, and the Russians provide some of their newest equipment there in order to test it. They have tested UAV [unmanned aerial vehicle] sensor-to-shooter techniques, et cetera, which are lethal. And so we need to continue to support them, in my view, to have the appropriate weapons to defend Ukraine.

Mr. SMITH. Thank you. Thank you, Mr. Chairman.

The CHAIRMAN. Mr. Wilson.

Mr. WILSON. Thank you, Mr. Chairman.

And, General, thank you very much. I have had the extraordinary opportunity to visit with you and I know firsthand your extraordinary dedication and success, and it is just heartwarming as the proud dad of three sons in the Army. I particularly appreciate—even one in the Navy—we appreciate you and just thank you so much.

With your service on the European Command and your previous assignment, of all things, to United States Forces Korea, you faced extraordinary challenges. Sadly, with the—so many permanently assigned forces not in your command currently now, how is this being addressed? And do you feel that we have enough military assets regionally to properly deter Russian aggression against the NATO alliance?

What other forces in particular do you need to properly deter any aggression? In addition, would the presence of these forces be accepted and welcomed in Europe?

General SCAPARROTTI. Well, thank you very much. It is good to see you again.

And within Europe we can do our job today. We can deter the Russian force that we see. We can counter terrorism, which is a part—a key part of our mission. We can enable our partners.

But if you look at the environment today and how it is evolving, and particularly the modernization I mentioned with Russia and the creativity of our—of the terrorists that we face as well, we need to ensure that we build a force that is relevant to that threat and can continue to deter.

So for those things that I need, one, it is—you know, I need intelligence, surveillance, and reconnaissance in greater numbers than I have now because to deter properly I have to be able to have a good baseline of Russia in particular so that I know when things change, I can posture my forces properly. So I need increased ISR to have good indications and warning and be able to set that posture properly over time.

Land force capabilities, which I mentioned earlier, but it is particularly the enablers of an armored division, a fires brigade, an engineer brigade, air defense, those kinds of systems in the numbers that I need there and as we move forward—now done on a rotational basis, but perhaps a rotational enduring or some mix of that.

Increased naval capabilities. It would be helpful to have a carrier support group and amphibious forces more than I have them now. I have them rotational as they go to other combatant commands. An increase of that would help us in deterrence; it would help us reinforce our interoperability with our partners and work with our partners.

And particularly I have noted ASW, antisubmarine warfare, because of the advances that Russia in particular is making in the undersea domain.

Enhanced missile defense. As we have seen every place in the world, ballistic missiles are proliferating and that is a very tough area.

And then finally, munitions, both modernization and appropriate stockpile, so that I have what we need if deterrence fails and we have to respond to crisis.

Mr. WILSON. Thank you for being so specific.

I am concerned that the military as a whole is facing a stark readiness crisis. Funding for training, maintenance and repair, new equipment, and future development of equipment has been short.

Aside from the aforementioned additional forces you may need, what shortfalls are you in particular seeing in your command? Please assess the readiness, the challenges of the European Command, and what resources are required to increase readiness in your area of responsibility.

General SCAPARROTTI. Well, I think, first of all when it comes to readiness I am fortunate in that particularly rotational forces, both Air Force, Army, Navy, et cetera, they are ready when they deploy. They come to me as a ready force.

And I would tell you that they depart as ready or more ready when they leave Europe because of our ability and training capacity there. So we are good in that area.

That is still, though, given the budget today and the demand against the OPTEMPO [operations tempo], as well as modernization that the services face, you know, increased funding, particularly for our pilots, would increase their capabilities within Europe. It would be helpful even at this point to increase their capability to fly more. That is both Army, that is Air Force as well.

When you go to our support within Europe, you know, we have been underfunding all the facilities that support not only our forces but support our families. And that is another area that as we look at—it is function of readiness as well, and it is something that today we don't fully fund and would be helpful to the force, too.

Mr. WILSON. And I want to thank you.

Another question concluding, the European Deterrence Initiative is very important, been very successful. And I know the South Carolina Army National Guard is grateful that we had a unit just leave for Poland, so thank you for your success.

The CHAIRMAN. General, just so I am clear, when you list ISR, antisubmarine warfare, missile defense, those are things you need more of, correct?

General SCAPARROTTI. They are things that I need more of. And, we also, when we get into the classified section I can talk to each of those in terms of capabilities and advancement we need to make, given modernization of our adversaries.

The CHAIRMAN. Okay. Thank you. I just wanted to be clear.

General SCAPARROTTI. That is correct.

The CHAIRMAN. Ms. Gabbard.

Mr. Norcross.

She didn't want to.

I am sorry, you are good? You want to wait? Okay.

Ms. Hanabusa.

Ms. HANABUSA. Thank you, Mr. Chair. And thank you, General.

General, I am kind of curious, I mean, I was here for the 2014 QDR [Quadrennial Defense Review] and, you know, it is sort of like how we set the tone, and I don't recall in that QDR or the QDR before that that I had an opportunity to review—I was not here for that—that there was a major concern about Russia.

And, matter of fact, I thought the philosophy was more along the lines that we thought we could kind of bring them around and they would become an ally of us. Then it seems like something occurred and all of a sudden they are viewed by some as our greatest threat.

So can you explain to me, General, how we go from thinking that maybe they will maybe be part of NATO, and all of a sudden it is like we have got to protect NATO and protect the 51 countries that are really part of EUCOM's AOR?

General SCAPARROTTI. Well, yes. I think prior to 2014—as I said, the transition that we are making in Europe right now is one from engagement and cooperation to deterrence and defense. And we made that—what the real trigger was—I mean, we began to see the modernization and where Russia was going prior to that, but 2014 the annexation of Crimea, the occupation of Ukraine, for instance, was enacted, clearly set out that we have Russia as a competitor that is willing and did break international law. And I think what you see in their activities today often is pushing wherever they can against the international norms.

They still occupy Ukraine and Georgia, for instance, with troops without invitation. We have seen their activities in cyber that are, at a minimal, criminal, in some cases: an attack on the Ukrainian power grid; most recently, Latvia believes they were a part of an attack on their government web system; and then their attempt to influence or inside of our election, and probably France and Germany, and others.

So I think, you know, if you look at their action it tells us that we have a nation here that we need to be very sober about. We don't seek conflict with them. Deterrence, in fact, has its mission to prevent conflict or war. But at this point Russia has not been very responsive to the international community in advancing Ukraine, Crimea, et cetera.

Ms. HANABUSA. So, General, what is your strategy that you would propose to this body as to what is necessary to prepare for Russia, whatever they may or you may be afraid that they are going to do? I think we like to have some sort of certainty of what—you know, what do you think the most probable scenario would be, and what is then what you need to have?

General SCAPARROTTI. Well, for example, I think Russia will continue to press against the international norms. They want to regain great power status, and the actions they are taking, in their view, is to ensure that.

What we need to do is we need to demonstrate strength. We need to be strong. That is what Russia respects.

They are opportunistic. Where they see weakness they will take advantage of it when it is in their interest.

We need a whole-of-government approach to this. It is not, in fact, the military is not the major part; it is the smaller part of this. We exist as a postured force to really provide muscle to our diplomacy, to information, to economics, et cetera.

We need to invest in the capabilities to make sure that we have a relevant force. A part of deterrence is, you know, the capability, and the credibility, and the final thing is communication. And I think communication with Russia is an important part to play in this.

Finally, strengthen our partners.

Ms. HANABUSA. General, do you believe that the concept of the triad and, you know, basically our nuclear forces is part of that deterrence structure that you need to have in the EUCOM?

General SCAPARROTTI. Yes, I do. I think the triad, as it exists in a safe and credible nuclear deterrent, is very important, particularly given Russia's capabilities.

Ms. HANABUSA. Do you think that is the only force that Russia understands, or would respect, I guess is the word?

General SCAPARROTTI. Yes. I think that they do focus on the strength of their opponent, and I think they are optimistic. Where they see weakness and they believe that they can gain their interest or objectives, they will move out on that.

Ms. HANABUSA. Thank you, Mr. Chair. I yield back.

The CHAIRMAN. Mr. Turner.

Mr. TURNER. Thank you, Mr. Chairman.

General, good to see you again. Thank you for your efforts in keeping us safe and helping us to plan for the defense of the United States and our allies.

Thank you for your strong statement on the issue of arming Ukraine. Congress has passed very strong resolutions calling for the same, including authorizing arming of Ukraine, so I appreciate your assessment of that circumstance and the advice that they bear investing in with the defensive armament.

As you know, I am very active in the NATO Parliamentary Assembly. I appreciate your participation with NATO Parliamentary Assembly. Several members of the Armed Services Committee are very active in that.

You know, it gives us an opportunity to interface with members of the various parliaments of the 28 nations. Recently we had a group of parliamentarians into Washington and we invited RAND in to conduct a military exercise based upon the RAND Russia-Baltics report that exposed the vulnerability of our Baltic NATO members. It was intriguing because a lot of the time that we spent on the presentation was informing our partners of Russia's current military posture, deployment, and capability.

So I would like you to talk for a minute about how do you keep our NATO partners informed, and is that a part of what you have to do of informing our partners of Russia's posture and the threat from Russia? Also then, if you would talk about if you believe that the forward-stationing of an armored brigade combat team in Europe on a permanent basis rather than rotational would be helpful in your deterrence quest.

And could you also give us just a brief discussion of how you have seen that the European Reassurance Initiative, our effort to pre-position equipment and to reassure our allies, has transitioned over the past year.

Thank you.

General SCAPARROTTI. Well, first of all, it is one of my responsibilities to work with our allies, both as EUCOM commander to the 51 nations, but specifically as the SACEUR [Supreme Allied Commander, Europe] and NATO command with the 28 nations.

We do that through a number of means: personal visits of myself and other leaders; information to the North Atlantic Council; exercises within the—within Europe, either with partners and/or NATO. And we invite leadership—political leadership, as well, to those.

And then finally, we do CMX, or a crisis management exercise, that brings in the leadership in NATO about every couple years, probably similar to what you experienced, in order to inform them of not only the capability of our adversaries, but the nature of war today.

You know, it is—decision space is much tighter. Information moves much faster. Those are the kinds of things, too, that I think it is helpful to discuss with the leadership.

Secondly, in terms of a—the rotational brigade, I would prefer to have an enduring armed force in Europe. That is a service decision. They provide right now is a rotational force; I would prefer to have an enduring one because the force then becomes accustomed to the environment, it forms relationships with our allies, they become well known over the period of time of several years that our service members are then stationed there, and have a greater appreciation for the problem set.

And then finally, within ERI: ERI is advancing very well, and thank this committee for your support of that. Without ERI we would not be postured to deter today as I have said we are.

It is what has allowed us to improve that posture today with a rotational brigade there with the ability to reinforce NATO with one of the Enhanced Forward Presence [EFP] battle groups from the U.S. and Poland, with additional support with air and naval forces. We have used it to improve infrastructure so that we can move forces into Europe and around Europe, and station forces in a more flexible, agile way.

All of those things have made a significant difference, and they also make a difference to our allies because we don't do this alone. We do this as an—you know, as an alliance, and just as our battle group will have a Romanian contingent with it and others, that is common when we train in Europe, as well.

Mr. TURNER. Thank you, General.

The aspect of informing our partners—it is very interesting to me because this is their neighborhood, but yet it seems like the United States still takes a lead on allowing our European partners to understand what their threats are and what the posture in the European arena is.

General SCAPARROTTI. Well, part of this—and I think it isn't just Europe, you know, the environment has changed; the nature of warfare has changed. And so it is easy sometimes not to realize that and then realize what the impacts of those changes are.

So that is the importance of doing the CMX, of getting out and keeping our allies informed and then, you know, our—both our military and our policy leaders have to also engage in that so that they learn, as well, because this environment is continuing to change and it has dramatically since 2014, for instance.

Mr. TURNER. Thank you. Mr. Chairman, I yield back.

The CHAIRMAN. Mr. Carbajal.

Mr. CARBAJAL. Thank you, Mr. Chair.

General Scaparrotti, you state that Russia is now the top theater priority. The Secretary of Defense has stated that Russia's aggressive actions have violated international law and are destabilizing. The message to this committee has been consistent: that Putin and the Russian Federation seek to disrupt the international order and the cohesion of the international organizations like NATO and EU [European Union].

You stated in your testimony that deterring Russia's—deterring Russia requires a whole-of-government approach. Unfortunately, I do not believe we have used a whole-of-government approach, especially as this branch of government has refused to investigate Russia's effort to disrupt this country's democratic process.

General, there are not many who can supersede your expertise on Russia. Today you have presented this committee with strategies to confront the Russian threat militarily. However, I am sure that you agree that it will take more than just military strength to effectively combat a state that is undermining and threatening democracies globally, including America's.

General, can you provide this committee the type of whole-of-government approach necessarily—or necessary to effectively deter Russia?

General SCAPARROTTI. Thank you, sir.

Russia is an adversary that employs whole of government. We see them work politically; we see them use economics as leverage;

we see them use information to influence populations—some of that is disinformation, as well. And so for us to be effective we have to respond across all those domains, as well.

So as a government—and we did this during the Cold War—as a government we had overarching objectives with respect to the Soviet Union then, but we need overarching objectives today. We need some lead agencies, like a lead agency in information, that has authorities to integrate across the different agencies in the government with respect to information. We need to approach them economically with the same overarching objectives.

So, you know, it is a very general description but that is literally where we need to go, every agency focused on our approach to Russia. And again, it is to influence them and not to have conflict, but to avoid conflict with them and yet protect our interests.

Mr. CARBAJAL. Do you find that we are being effective?

General SCAPARROTTI. I would say that we are not as effective as we could be. We can organize, particularly as whole of government, in a better way, and I believe we will. I think that at least my leadership and what I know is focused on that, and we have work to do.

So we can be more effective, particularly in the information domain where, you know, we have, I think, very good capability, good talent, creativity, and we just need to move out on that a bit.

Mr. CARBAJAL. And not to make it so simplistic, but what could this Congress do to address the highest priority that perhaps is our weakest link in being more effective?

General SCAPARROTTI. Well, I think provide the leadership in those objectives. Provide the leadership toward a, you know, a cohesive, integrated governmental approach to this problem. And then as you do, finance those efforts, as well.

Mr. CARBAJAL. Thank you. Thank you very much. I yield back, Mr. Chair.

The CHAIRMAN. Mr. Wittman.

Mr. WITTMAN. Thank you, Mr. Chairman.

General Scaparrotti, thanks again. Appreciate you joining us here, and thanks again for your service. It has always been an honor to visit you when we have had the opportunity in places like Korea and elsewhere.

I wanted to ask you about the mission of the Enhanced Forward Presence battalions that are located in the Baltic nations and Poland. Can you give us a little laydown about what those units are there training and preparing to do? And do these battalions effectively deter Russia? How does Russia look at that with a total force presence there?

Obviously, with Russian forces along the border there in the Baltic nations—as we visited the Baltic nations they are deeply concerned about the presence of armor artillery units and Russian troops stationed along the border.

Does our presence there with these Enhanced Forward Presence units—is that a significant deterrence? And how do we use those units in coordination with our allies, both in training and in presence?

General SCAPARROTTI. The Enhanced Forward Presence is a—in NATO terms they call it a battle group. It is a battalion task force.

Mr. WITTMAN. Yes.

General SCAPARROTTI. But it is combined with—in Poland with Polish troops. We have Romanian troops as a part of that, and others. And we operate with Polish forces in the defense of their nation.

It is under NATO operational control. It is a very significant force. I think it has a significant impact on deterrence.

This is a very strong commitment from the 28 nations of NATO that they are—that they will honor Article 5, that an attack on one nation is an attack on all. And so while some may say, "Well, it is four battalion task forces," it is four battalion task forces but it is a statement that is backed by 28 nations and all of their capability—not just military, but economic, informational, et cetera.

Russia does respect NATO. It is one of the reasons that they are trying to undermine NATO and fracture it is because they do respect NATO. So I think it is effective.

The last thing I want to say is, is that while we do focus on a battle—a task force, it is connected to the other domains. You know, we connect with our air, our maritime, and those others that we can bring to bear. So we can fight it as we fight today.

Mr. WITTMAN. As I visited there our allies express two desires. One is increased U.S. presence as a permanent presence there in the Baltic States. And, of course, we talked to them about rotational presence, and I would try to convince them you actually have more troops there on a rotational presence that know your country and know operationally than you would if you had just a battalion. But they are all about, let's have a battalion presence there.

So I want to ask about how your conversations with our allies have gone about their view of our commitment and that element of presence. And then secondly, too, when Secretary Mattis went there and had a heart-to-heart discussion about the commitment that NATO nations need to make as far as funding their militaries, give me your perspective on whether you see that commitment growing.

Is it growing in the right ways to make sure that they are working with us to create that presence and that deterrence? And how important is it in the minds of many of our allies there for that permanent presence, which, as you know, we have moved away from since the days of the Cold War?

General SCAPARROTTI. First of all, I just visited each of the Baltic countries a week ago, and in every country, as you said, they asked for permanent presence of U.S. forces. And I have said publicly that they have near-permanent presence of U.S. forces. It is rotational, but it is enduring.

Mr. WITTMAN. Right.

General SCAPARROTTI. And we are committed to that as long as these conditions exist.

The one upside of a rotational force is that we are bringing rotational forces through and much more of our force structure then becomes familiar with the environment——

Mr. WITTMAN. Yes.

General SCAPARROTTI [continuing]. The people, the challenges, their allies in Europe. That is a benefit to it.

And so, for instance, from the Army chief of staff's perspective that is very good for his force——

Mr. WITTMAN. Sure.

General SCAPARROTTI [continuing]. As you rotate different units through.

Mr. WITTMAN. Yes.

General SCAPARROTTI. And that is good for us. If we had to respond to a crisis we would certainly bring forces from the States to reinforce us.

I think they understand that. I would just say they are very appreciative of the United States contributions to their defense. There is no question about that.

In terms of funding growth, we have seen a change in NATO and a response. Last year was the first year that was—the trend was not down in terms of percent of funding of GDP across the 28 nations. It turned up.

This year it was an increase of 3.8 percent, I think it is, but 22 nations have increased their budget this year.

I said I was just in the Baltics, for instance. Estonia already meets the 2 percent; Lithuania and Latvia both told me they will meet it by 2018 and probably go beyond that.

So countries are responding. What is important to this, too, though, I would point out, is that we meet the 20 percent agreement for modernization——

Mr. WITTMAN. Yes.

General SCAPARROTTI [continuing]. Because they have to be a relevant force, as well.

Mr. WITTMAN. Right. Very good. Thank you, Mr. Chairman. I yield back.

The CHAIRMAN. Mr. Brown.

Mr. BROWN. Thank you, Mr. Chairman.

And, General, thank you for your presence here. Thank you for your service and your leadership in Europe.

A few decades ago I had the privilege of serving with 180,000 or so Army personnel when we defended the Fulda Gap. We won the Cold War.

A lot has changed since then. I participated in a lot of interoperability exercises, Reforger and a number of others, with, you know, French and British and German forces. And we relied a lot on their infrastructure, particularly the transportation and communication network.

My question has to do with that infrastructure. You mentioned in your written testimony as well as, I think, you briefly touched upon it today, that the expansion of the alliance to include Central and European—Central and Eastern European countries has made it a little more challenging with the lack of a common transportation network.

So as you anticipate what could be a Russian aggression on the eastern flank of NATO, could you briefly describe some of the challenges that you would have in feasibly moving both U.S. and NATO forces along or across multiple sovereign countries and getting the permissions and the support—roads, bridges, rail, and the like?

General SCAPARROTTI. Yes. In the days that you trained there— and I trained there, as well—we had a very good basis and understanding of the—of mobility, whether it is rail, air, ground, bridge construction, weight that it would take. We had a very good under-standing of Europe and how to move our force.

Over the years of partnership, the last 20 years or so, we began to atrophy that. We don't have as good an understanding of our road networks, and particularly those nations that were once a part of Warsaw Pact to the east that are now partners with us.

So we are developing that and we are working that hard with our partners. The alliance countries are doing a lot. Germany, in particular, has been very helpful.

But we are having to take a look at do we have the rail capacity? Are the bridges strong enough, and which ones can we move across? Those kinds of things.

And with EFP and our rotational brigade, those two in par-ticular, we have been exercising that.

Final thing I would like to say is the allies contributed to this. They are all becoming a part of mobility and infrastructure that we need to have an agile force in Europe.

Mr. BROWN. And can you state whether or not we currently or— and if not, whether we should be making any investments in that infrastructure, considering the security interests that we have?

General SCAPARROTTI. We are currently making investments in that, as well as our allies, and we should continue to do that.

We have to have some agility. We won't know exactly how things may roll out if there is a crisis nor where it may happen. We are routinely not as good at being very precise in that determination in the future.

So we have to develop infrastructure and mobility within Europe that allows us a good deal of agility. And then we need to train against that, as well, and exercise it.

Mr. BROWN. Thank you. I yield back, Mr. Chairman.

The CHAIRMAN. Mr. Scott.

Mr. SCOTT. Thank you, Mr. Chairman.

General, good to see you again. Part of my questions revolve around rail, the difference in the gauges, the fact that our equip-ment is so large now that it won't go through some of the tunnels that have been there for so long.

I will shift, then, to lift capacity—our large lift capacity. If we can't get our equipment there by rail or by tunnel, do we have the lift capacity, with the retirement of the C–5s that we have had in the last couple of years, that we would need? And do we have the ability to land those planes with their weight where we would need the equipment?

General SCAPARROTTI. As you can imagine, we are looking at all this with respect to our plans. STRATCOM [U.S. Strategic Com-mand] could probably give you the—or Transportation Command could give you the best response to that, but as I have conversed with them and we look at our plans, we can move. It is little slower than I might like at this point.

I am concerned about the future, in terms of the investment not only in military but also civilian ships and aircraft that we rou-tinely rely upon in a crisis. And in that area we need to continue investment or we will continually meet greater challenges here in the future, from what I have seen in our planning.

Mr. SCOTT. Yes, sir. I am concerned about that, as well. I think that the lift capacity, especially large lift capacity, is something that we need to revisit.

We talked about the JSTARS [Joint Surveillance Target Attack Radar System] in Europe. I have very serious concerns about is the number of units we have go in for major overhauls, major depot maintenance, that you would potentially end up with a shortage of that. Do you see the demand for JSTARS decreasing? And what effects are there if there is a moving target indicator gap?

General SCAPARROTTI. This is particularly important against a large force like Russia so that we do have good information, we understand movement and change. That is how we build the indications and warnings [I&W] and the ability to react appropriately, so it is very important to us.

I am concerned about the reduction as we bring on new aircraft, which we need to do. I do not have all that I would like to have today to provide the I&W that I need in Europe.

Mr. SCOTT. As we discuss the upcoming budget, potential decreases in funding to the State Department are a concern, I think, of most of the people on this committee.

How much more difficult does this make your mission? And what challenges do you face with these potential shortcomings in the budget? And how does it potentially hurt our partnerships in the region?

General SCAPARROTTI. Well, you know, I—in terms of where the budget is at is not in—mine to comment on, but I would say that, as I noted earlier, our problems—all the problems that we face in Europe require a whole-of-government approach and they require, you know, approach with partners in the same fashion.

So if you look at how I counter transnational threats or terrorism inside of Europe, military is a part of that; we have that cell that runs that in EUCOM, but most of the work is done by Treasury, State, and others across our agencies to complete that work and enable us to do it.

And again, I think that in deterring Russia it is a whole-of-government approach, as well. Diplomacy should be the priority and we, as a military, with the right posture, provide some muscle for diplomacy to work.

Mr. SCOTT. General, I appreciate your service. And with that, Mr. Chairman, I yield the remainder of my time.

The CHAIRMAN. Mrs. Murphy.

Mrs. MURPHY. General Scaparrotti, thank you for being here today.

I want to start by noting that I have deep concerns about the current administration's continued publicly questioning of our alliances and the sanctity of the post-World War II international order. I think it is a dangerous narrative that reflects both an internal and external threat to our national security.

Externally, the rise of Russian aggression in the—and Russia's use of hybrid warfare tactics are directly intended to erode the credibility of U.S. leadership in the world. And internally here at home there is a growing sentiment that we should withdraw from the world.

Isolationism resonates in our own country with people who are worried about their livelihoods being taken away by increasingly interconnected world and who are increasingly weary of being involved in a protracted conflict overseas. But this view is populist and perilous.

You know well, though, that our alliances help prevent larger conflict around the world every day and shore up our security at home. And in your testimony you have spoken a lot about the successes of the European Reassurance Initiative, or ERI, to reassure our allies and deter regional aggression.

What policies, authorities, capabilities have been particularly useful in the success of ERI? And then what authorities and investments do you still need to complement the ERI efforts, especially in the emerging cyber domain?

General SCAPARROTTI. Yes, thank you very much.

In terms of ERI, the focal areas have been the rotational force presence that we have, so it supports that rotational brigade—armored brigade; it supports the rotational combat aviation brigade; it supports our Enhanced Forward Presence, the battle group in Poland.

It supports an expansion and pre-positioning of stops—stocks of the airfields that we will have available to use day to day and in a crisis. It provides the pre-positioning of stocks for Army forces so that I can build combat power that is not in Europe if I need to in a crisis.

It has enhanced our training and interoperability with our allies. We are doing—I wouldn't say more necessarily; we are doing better exercises that are integrated with allies and reinforce interoperability that is relevant to the adversaries that we will face.

It has helped us with antisubmarine warfare, for instance, which is another area that I noted. So it is very important.

I would tell you, as I look to the future I will continue to need it for those same reasons and more. But it will be across all the services and it will tackle the correct posture that I need and the capabilities that I need to deter Russia.

Finally, I didn't mention infrastructure, although I have said it several times. It has been fundamental in making infrastructure upgrades in airfields, bases, and other places that enable the movement of not only our forces but the allies, as well.

Mrs. MURPHY. And then, given your experience as the commander of U.S. Forces Korea, do you think that the ERI model can be effectively exported to the Asia-Pacific region to deter provocative and aggressive behavior from actors like North Korea and China?

General SCAPARROTTI. You know, really it comes down to specified funding. And to me it would be—it certainly could be a concept used in the Pacific, but I think what is important, and what is important even within ERI, is that we have, you know, a predictable funding into the future because really, as a military that is most helpful. It allows us to plan ahead and set objectives in the future and know that we will be funded to reach that and set the readiness that we need.

Mrs. MURPHY. Thank you, sir. And I yield back the remainder of my time.

The CHAIRMAN. Mr. Cook.

Mr. COOK. Thank you, Mr. Chairman. It is good to see you again, General. I was there with Chris Gibson last summer.

Just like when we met in Korea, you are very, very candid. Your comments about the U–2 in Korea and some of the last time on readiness I thought gave us great insight into what is going on.

We were there, one of things I was concerned about is—I don't know how you sleep at night. I asked you the same thing, I think, in Korea. I think you just have more nightmares in this new job than the last one, but we won't go there—because I have my own; I am in Congress.

Anyway, the pre-positions—I am concerned about obviously the RAND study, the T–14, the modernization of the T–90, et cetera, et cetera, et cetera. And when we were there we went out and looked at some of the pre-positioning that had changed, and obviously, like the gentleman that had asked you that question about the Fulda Gap years ago, boy, we don't have that many troops in our pre-positioned forces. We have to go a long, long ways.

And looking at some of the warehouses and the condition, I knew it was bad but I didn't think it was that bad. And can you comment? Am I just being alarmist about one of 20 different things and—but I share those—I don't think we are going to have the lift, everything else, if we don't have pre-positioned forces and equipment there. I think we are going to be behind the power curve.

General SCAPARROTTI. We can deal with the challenges we have today with the posture we have, but it is at increased risk. And it is increased risk. If we have a conflict it is going to be increased casualties, it is going to take more time, et cetera.

I will sleep more comfortably as our posture improves. And that is why ERI is so important; that is why getting, you know, the pre-post stocks that you mentioned in place is important; it is why, you know, the service chiefs are focused on readiness today to ensure that we have got forces that are ready for the challenges they face with a—you know, with a peer like—with an adversary like Russia.

So we have got a good deal of work to do. In the closed session I can be more frank about those things that are most concerning to me.

Mr. COOK. I am going to switch gears a little. I am going to put on partly a foreign affairs hat.

Montenegro, the vote yesterday was 98–2 in the Senate. It looks like that is going forward. And from a military standpoint I think you know about the designs of Russia on that country and the importance of that country militarily and politically in NATO. So I was optimistic.

How do you think the possibilities, whether that is going to happen—and obviously this is going to give you another nightmare or headache or what have you, but I was one of those ones pushing for Montenegro.

General SCAPARROTTI. Well, I think we have two nations, one of which is ours, to confirm that within the alliance, so I expect fully that they will be. I think it is critical that Montenegro does become a part of the alliance, as is planned.

For Russia, this is something they did not want to see happen. As you know, they went to great lengths to try and undermine Montenegro's accession to NATO.

So I think it is critical that this occurs. And I have said before, I think that Russia has every objective of ensuring that there is not another country that joins NATO in the future. I think that is their objective.

Mr. COOK. Once again, I want to thank you so much. Looking forward to seeing you again over there. And I yield back.

The CHAIRMAN. Mr. Suozzi.

Mr. SUOZZI. Thank you, Mr. Chairman.

General, I want to add my voice to the chorus of praise for the great work that you have devoted your life to, and we are very grateful to you for your service, and you really do have an awesome responsibility.

I am new to this and I am very concerned about the things that aren't easy to measure. You know it is easier—and you are doing a great job—to measure troop movements and hardware and things like that, but in your testimony you talk about, "Russia has employed a decades-long strategy of indirect action to coerce, destabilize, and otherwise exercise a malign influence over other nations." And you talk about the neighboring states of Moldova and Georgia and the Balkans.

And then you say, "Additional Russian activities short of war range from disinformation to manipulation. Examples include Russia's outright denial of involvement in the lead up to Russia's occupation and attempted annexation of Crimea; attempts to influence elections in the United States, France, and elsewhere; its aggressive propaganda campaigns targeting ethnic Russian populations among its neighbors; and cyber activities directed against infrastructure in the Baltic nations and the Ukraine."

So everybody, I think, now agrees that Russia has been, you know—Ukraine was easy to see and what they did there was such a negative action; and the cyber threats, everybody agrees that that is a big part of their strategy these days; propaganda, influencing the media; Russian oligarchs spreading money around in all different places of the world, from Ukraine to Europe—European elections.

So when you talk about the whole-of-government approach, they are not as easy to measure these different things that they are doing.

I am a big advocate that we need to give some sort of punch in the nose, some sort of clear manifestation that, "We don't like what you are doing," and we need to go after the oligarchs with financial sanctions and try and pay more attention to sending a clear message that you can't mess with us that way.

What is the one thing that you would like to see the whole of government—really not just related to more hardware, more positioning of troops, more the things that you are advocating for— what is the one thing you would like to see the rest of government do to give them a strong message that you can't do this to us or you are going to have to pay a price?

General SCAPARROTTI. Well, I think the whole-of-government approach—I think one of the most important things we can do is get organized in the information campaign.

Mr. SUOZZI. Whose job is that?

General SCAPARROTTI. Well, you know, I think today the way it rests is with State traditionally has that. We have the GEC [Global Engagement Center]. But again, you know, they have to be resourced. We as a government have to say——

Mr. SUOZZI. This is a priority.

General SCAPARROTTI [continuing]. And it is a priority, and provide the integration, provide them the authority to integrate in a way that would have that effect.

But when you look at the way Russia is working today with disinformation, even the way that they approach different countries in Europe and in the public world on RT [Russian international TV network], Russian TV, et cetera, we have to compete in that environment. We have to compete in it.

We have to show strength that also supports our values. I think we ought to be very strong in our values in doing this, as well, and I think that would have a great effect.

It is interesting because in many countries in the East, even though they are doing all of this, there are countries that the populace is not necessarily swayed by what they hear from Russia.

Mr. SUOZZI. Yes.

General SCAPARROTTI. That is not true in all of them. It depends on where you are at, but it is interesting to me.

And yet, you know, if we made a greater—a, you know, a greater effort in this area, I think we could see some good benefit.

Mr. SUOZZI. So you would like to see some more strength from America as far as coordinating the information campaign, preferably using the State Department as they have traditionally done, to try and get this information out there and then send a message clearly back to them.

General SCAPARROTTI. Absolutely, and to work with our allies.

Mr. SUOZZI. I have 59 more seconds in my time, but I just wanted to say that, you know, I was speaking to the Italians. The Italians' biggest concern of the whole world right now is Libya. And, of course, that is the funnel where, you know, they have closed off through Turkey and now everybody is coming up through Libya.

What is it we should be doing to try and help stabilize Libya or to try and create an environment where that is less of a channel for people to be migrating from the rest of Africa and the surrounding region?

General SCAPARROTTI. Well, Libya is not a part of EUCOM. It is AFRICOM's [U.S. Africa Command's] domain.

What we are doing basically in EUCOM is to assist our allies with both the refugees that come from there and their—the challenges in Europe they have with that, as well as countering the transnational threats that are coming out of the instability in the north, as well.

Mr. SUOZZI. But you are hearing the same concerns from the Italians that that is their big concern is what is going on Libya?

General SCAPARROTTI. Yes, sir. I mean, if you go to the southern part of Europe the more imminent threat to them is—or challenge—I wouldn't say it is a threat; it is a challenge—it is the continued flow of refugees and the terrorist threat. Those two are more prominent than Russia.

If you go to the east of Europe it is obviously Russia. But all of those challenges are true for all the nations in Europe.

Mr. SUOZZI. Thank you, General.

The CHAIRMAN. Mr. Kelly.

Mr. KELLY. Thank you, Mr. Chairman. And thank you, General Scaparrotti, for being here.

I have two questions so I would like to kind of contain the first one to the first 2.5 minutes so I can get into the second.

This committee has consistently supported ERI and now EDI [European Deterrence Initiative]. In fact, last year we tried to shift a large portion of the EDI to base budget funding.

One of the reasons is that by budgeting through OCO [Overseas Contingency Operations] we don't have a complete FYDP [Future Years Defense Program] for EDI so we can't plan and we can't see how you are planning for these activities. In fact, I can't think of much that would concern Putin more than to see a 5-year EDI plan and budget.

Can you provide the committee with your best military advice on what an EDI FYDP would look like, broken down by budget activity, before we mark up the fiscal year 2018 NDAA [National Defense Authorization Act]?

General SCAPARROTTI. Sir, when we in EUCOM have produced our request for ERI we have done it in a very deliberate fashion based on the guidance from Congress as to what ERI's purpose is across all of the services that support me and EUCOM. And so it is a detailed list.

We scrubbed it against things like—you know, we questioned ourselves: Is this something that really ought to be in base or ought to be a service expense, not a part of ERI?

So I think we did a very faithful job of that and provided it to OSD [Office of the Secretary of Defense], and we can certainly, you know, break that out in terms of we not only had the categories but also the prioritization that we provided OSD, as well. And assuming that there is no issue there, I can tell you we have done the work.

Mr. KELLY. And you agree that it is much better to have a 5-year plan rather than a 1-year and we don't know what the budget—baseline funding, as opposed to OCO, is much better for us to plan and also shows our allies our commitment. Would you agree, General?

General SCAPARROTTI. I, as I have said before, said that we need predictable long-term budgeting so that we can plan out ahead, as opposed to a year at a time.

Mr. KELLY. And thank you.

And I am an Old Guard member. I grew up in the 1980s. I grew up as part of the Reforgers and all those things in Europe.

When we had three ACRs [armored cavalry regiments], we had 2nd, 3rd and 11th—we may have had more—but those were our screening forces. Those weren't even talking about the divisions and corps behind them and our commitment to the European theater.

We no longer have that. I actually visited Hohenfels near Nuremberg last year and saw the difference in what it looked like in the 1980s versus now.

I am also a big, strong proponent of the National Guard and our Guard and Reserves. We have 8 National Guard divisions; we have 32 BCTs [brigade combat teams], of which 10 are armored, I believe, or heavy BCTs in the Guard and Reserve.

I also believe in what you said, General Scaparrotti, about having that continuous force over there that the people know and trust. So I think we need to look outside of how we have always done things or how we look and project.

If we kept one heavy BCT that is an Active Component over there and integrated a divisional rotation from the National Guard of maybe two heavy and one light or, you know, one heavy with another heavy plus a light, it gives training opportunities to those division headquarters; it gives terrain familiarity; it gives so many things.

What do you think about that, and including also like your engineer and your ADA [air defense artillery] and your aviation assets, to go with those Guard divisions on maybe a 5-year—one division for 5 years—I mean for 1 year and then, you know, through a 5-year cycle.

General SCAPARROTTI. Well, you know, as I have said before, that is really a service function for them to determine. I make the requirement.

There are a number of ways that—as you said, there are a number of ways we can fulfill my requirement and there are pros and cons of each. And, you know, as you noted, rotational units provide a lot of experience to our force, and it provides a force that then has knowledge of Europe. So those are the advantages of that.

Mr. KELLY. And one other thing, I think you can look at deployment, your RSOI [reception, staging, onward movement, and integration], a little differently. Rather than having to send a Guard unit that is 100 percent ready on day one, if you send them to the European theater as a division those BCTs can actually get those rotations at Hohenfels and other places rather than at the NTC [National Training Center].

And so the end product is a completely trained and ready-to-fight division and BCTs, as opposed to sending one over there that is already ready. I think maybe you get to train and be ready across the spectrum. Would you agree with that?

General SCAPARROTTI. What I need is a trained and ready unit at the point of employment. So certainly we can use our capabilities in Europe if that is the most efficient way to get there.

And I would just add that, you know, the Guard plays an important role in what we do in Europe every day. The partnership that they have formed with each of the countries is really quite remarkable—20-some years of relationship that builds trust.

Mr. KELLY. Thank you. And I yield back, Mr. Chairman.

The CHAIRMAN. Mr. Gallego.

Mr. GALLEGO. Thank you, General.

First off—and we will be switching direction a couple times—do our European partners support the provision of lethal defense equipment to Ukraine?

General SCAPARROTTI. I haven't discussed that specific issue with most of our partners. As you know, there are some of our allies in Europe that are supporting Ukraine; they train right along beside us. So they are as convicted as we are in supporting Ukraine and the protection of their sovereignty. I can say that.

Mr. GALLEGO. And switching gears—thank you, General, for that answer—how should we holistically approach deterrence in our response to hybrid threats in Europe specifically from Russia? Are other measures such as sanctions effective in dealing with hybrid activity, or should we be looking at potentially a military response for some level of hybrid activity?

General SCAPARROTTI. First of all, I think, for instance, you mentioned sanctions. Again, I think that a response to Russia has to be a whole-of-government approach, and that is the economic part of that that is important that we retain.

As I have said, I think demonstrating strength in every area is significantly important with Russia. I think that we have got to have the right posture of our military.

And when you look at deterrence you look at capability, credibility, and then communication. And communication being, do we communicate our intent and our objective, and does Russia understand that so there is no miscalculation? And then a part of that military is an enhanced missile defense, as well.

Mr. GALLEGO. I yield back my time.

The CHAIRMAN. Mr. Rogers.

Mr. ROGERS. Thank you, Mr. Chairman. And, General, good to see you again. Thanks for being here and thank you for your service to our country.

I especially appreciated your comments earlier today about the United States needs to provide some lethal force capability to the Ukrainian military. I have been there twice and going back next month, and they are begging for something to fight with. And this is a life-or-death battle for them, so I appreciate your candor on that.

I want to talk to you first about the INF [Intermediate-Range Nuclear Forces Treaty]. In your best military professional judgment, do you believe that Russia in the foreseeable future will return to compliance with the INF Treaty?

General SCAPARROTTI. I don't have any indication that they will at this time.

Mr. ROGERS. How much longer do you think that the United States should continue to unilaterally comply with that treaty?

General SCAPARROTTI. Well, that is really a policy decision. What I would say is that, from my perspective, is that we have to respond to their violation of that treaty one way or the other. We have to take steps; we have to address it. But——

Mr. ROGERS. What steps would you take?

General SCAPARROTTI [continuing]. It is a policy matter.

Mr. ROGERS. What steps would you take? What would you recommend to the President that we take?

General SCAPARROTTI. Well, first of all, I think we confront them and then we consider what actions we might take in terms of our capabilities in order to deal with the advance that their violation of the treaty incurs—in other words, the risk that we are taking because they are not following that treaty and how do we respond to it.

Mr. ROGERS. Okay. I want to turn to the nuclear weapons ban. What are some of the military risks to the alliance and our allies if NATO members sign onto and thus comply with the draft of a U.N. [United Nations] nuclear weapons ban that is currently being negotiated?

General SCAPARROTTI. My view is that the nuclear weapons ban is just not realistic. I mean it is occurring in a world where we have North Korea, in particular, who is in violation of U.N. sanctions and resolutions—multiple ones—and show no respect for the international community's directive; Russia, who is also aggressively improving their modernization of their nuclear weapons, et cetera.

So I think we are in a world today where that is just not realistic at this point.

I think it is something that probably all of us would like to see and, you know, a world without nuclear weapons. But I don't think we are at the point to exercise that ban at this time.

Mr. ROGERS. Do you believe that it would be inconsistent for NATO members who have signed on to the Warsaw Communiqué to also sign on to that treaty?

General SCAPARROTTI. Again, that is each nation's sovereign decision, but I think it would be.

Mr. ROGERS. Thank you. I yield back, Mr. Chairman.

The CHAIRMAN. Mr. Garamendi.

Mr. GARAMENDI. There are a lot of questions we ought to get to here and probably quickly to the classified hearing, so I am going to be very quick.

Our new President has created considerable concern about the role of the United States vis-a-vis the European Union and NATO. Has that uncertainty caused you problems in your work as NATO—with NATO?

General SCAPARROTTI. No. Our mil-to-mil relationships within the alliance are strong. We have continued to do what we need to do as an alliance of military components to protect the transatlantic region.

Mr. GARAMENDI. Is there clarity in your mind as to what the administration's policy is with regard to NATO?

General SCAPARROTTI. The Secretary of Defense attended the last defense ministers [meeting] and had sat through 2 days of sessions and was very clear in terms of America's commitment to NATO as well as in Munich at the Munich Security Conference. And the Vice President spoke there, as well. So I think that they were very clear in our commitment to NATO.

Mr. GARAMENDI. Well, that is not the entire story, is it? There are other people that have commented in various ways.

General SCAPARROTTI. What I would say, Congressman, is that there has been uncertainty throughout our election, et cetera, that the Secretary and the Vice President spoke on behalf of the administration. I do believe that Secretary Tillerson's attendance at the foreign ministry—at the foreign ministers conference coming up, as well as the President's attendance in May, will reinforce our commitment.

Mr. GARAMENDI. Is it important in your work that there be clarity from the administration with regard to its commitment to NATO and Europe?

General SCAPARROTTI. Yes.

Mr. GARAMENDI. Well, we will hopefully have that in the near future.

Down into the weeds for a few moments, you mentioned the issue of being able to move material and troops and the role of the civilian organizations in doing that. We have a hearing coming up at the end of this week with TRANSCOM [U.S. Transportation Command], and specifically on the issue of ships, the Ready Reserve, and the MSP [Maritime Security Program].

Do you see the—are—do we have sufficient ships, planes, to address any contingency that you might face as your role in EUCOM?

General SCAPARROTTI. Again, that is best answered by them, but I can tell you from my experience in the past year and a half that they and I have concern about particularly our civilian support in both ships and air, and that we have to invest in those.

I haven't recently sat down with them to get the actual facts, but that is my view in dealing with the planning that we are—we have done.

Mr. GARAMENDI. Well, your last two commands have been at the far ends of the world, so you would know. I think I will let it go at that point.

Thank you, and I yield back my time.

The CHAIRMAN. Ms. Stefanik.

Ms. STEFANIK. Thank you, Mr. Chairman. And thank you, General Scaparrotti, for your leadership.

You and I have had the opportunity to discuss the importance of countering Russian propaganda and malign influence in the information space, and during our last conversation you mentioned the Russia Information Group, which is a working-level interagency group to counter Russian aggression. And I am pleased to see the efforts of this group and the State Department's Global Engagement Center.

But my question for you is: What aren't we doing that we need to be doing in this area to more effectively counter Russian propaganda? We discussed a lot of the improvements that have been made in terms of grappling with this issue, but what more do we need to be doing?

General SCAPARROTTI. Well, I think, you know, we do have a structure. We have the group that you mentioned, for instance, that is multiagency, et cetera.

But we actually have to, you know, provide it direction and resourcing on a larger scale than has been done to this point. That is the first thing.

Second thing is I think we have to be more direct in our values and our messaging. If we think back to Voice of America, there is— in Europe today there are those in the eastern countries that tell me that they recall when they were in the Warsaw Pact hearing

Voice of America and the difference it made. Those are the kind of things we need to do on a greater scale than we are doing today.

Ms. STEFANIK. So let me ask you this: As you know, in last year's NDAA we expanded the mandate of the Global Engagement Center, which is within the State Department, to include state-sponsored entities of propaganda such as Russia. How can we empower the Global Engagement Center? And a larger question is, is that the right coordinating body within the State Department?

General SCAPARROTTI. Again, I think whether that is the right coordinating body I think is probably best determined by the State Department, not I. I really can't tell you best how they should organize for this.

But I think it is a good start. It is an agency that we know we can go to that is empowered within State to conduct this mission.

And so, again, my experience with it is that this is on a much smaller scale than we need today. We have an opportunity here, I think, to focus on this. And perhaps with a new administration, et cetera, we can begin to empower that more and reinforce it.

And whether that is exactly the way it should be, I think we will see as time goes on.

Ms. STEFANIK. You mentioned in your response to some of the other questions the importance of working with our partners. What can we do to better leverage more the NATO Strategic Communication Center of Excellence in Latvia, similar to the way that EUCOM and NATO leverage the NATO Special Operations Headquarters?

General SCAPARROTTI. Yes. We in EUCOM are actually connecting with that node. We in EUCOM are connecting with EU and NATO, for instance.

So what we are trying to do is form nodes, and on the cyber side that is a very important one in Estonia. And then, through that, reinforce this network that defeats a network, so to speak. That is what we have to do. And so we are working—I mean, that is one of our basic models within EUCOM to empower that.

And, on the NATO side, they have approved a strategic direction, is what I would call it there, that enables parts of our chain of command within NATO to link with EUCOM's command.

So I think there are the beginnings of this. We just need to begin to reinforce it and develop it.

Ms. STEFANIK. And my last question is, 2 years ago in the fiscal year 2016 NDAA this committee noted concern about hybrid and unconventional threats and directed DOD to submit a strategy for countering unconventional and hybrid threats. Unfortunately, the DOD has yet to submit or even begin to coordinate with other government agencies.

In our language in the NDAA we also noted that, quote, "Most state sponsors of unconventional warfare, such as Russia and Iran, have doctrinally linked conventional warfare, economic warfare, cyber warfare, information operations, intelligence operations, and other activities seamlessly in an effort to undermine U.S. national security objectives and the objectives of U.S. allies alike."

First, do you agree with this assessment still and the need to develop such a comprehensive whole-of-government strategy? And second, in terms of countering hybrid warfare, are we any closer to linking all of our tools and capabilities?

General SCAPARROTTI. I agree that we have to have a holistic, whole-of-government strategy, as you stated. I think we are closer. I think we, you know, we are not sitting still; we are making progress.

And particularly, I can speak to the military side of this. As I said, we are working with our allies through established nodes. Our special operations forces, in particular, are very good at this and they are active, not only in what they can provide us in this domain but also building capacity with our allies.

Ms. STEFANIK. Thank you.

The CHAIRMAN. Mr. Larsen.

Mr. LARSEN. Thanks, Mr. Chairman. General, welcome.

I have a question to clarify some Pentagon math I am trying to figure out. It goes—and maybe you can help—it goes back to your comments about wanting a division in EUCOM. So I am trying to figure out, were you suggesting that you wanted an additional brigade on top of the two brigades to get to a division, or are you suggesting an additional division on top of two brigades?

General SCAPARROTTI. Yes. I am suggesting an additional division, because what I need is I need armored and mech [mechanized] brigades. The two I have there today are, you know, a cavalry, light cav, as well as an airborne infantry brigade combat team.

Mr. LARSEN. Yes. And then along with that, a headquarters, presumably?

General SCAPARROTTI. Yes, and the enablers. But the reason a division is so important is because it is at that level you can then have the command and control, communications, capability to integrate the different domains in the way we fight. And then that division brings the enablers, like appropriate artillery, engineers, air defense, et cetera, that fill out a proper defense.

Mr. LARSEN. And then does that—does your concept then come with additional pre-positioned forces—or equipment, that is, pre-positioned equipment? Are we looking at supporting the division with pre-po or equipment coming with the division itself?

General SCAPARROTTI. Today the pre-position stocks that we are building are an integral part of that division so that it would—so that people would fly over, fall in on, and I would have a division filling that out. So that is the plan today. The plan today is a rotational brigade, and then a pre-po that provides the remainder of the resources.

Mr. LARSEN. All right, thanks. Thanks for clarifying that. Appreciate it. Pentagon math, sometimes pretty easy.

Can you talk about a little bit the high north? There are some comments in your written testimony on Russia's investment in its area of the Arctic, which there is some rational basis to that because as the ice recedes they no longer—nor can much of anyone—rely on the ice to sort of protect your surface.

We are active in the Arctic Council—the U.S., along with Russia and Norway and five other countries, as active members of the Arctic Council, and a lot of observers, as well. Just kind of what—since it is mentioned in your written testimony about the high north, what do you suggest from a EUCOM perspective, or even from a NATO perspective, would be an appropriate response?

General SCAPARROTTI. Yes, sir. I agree that, you know, we have typically looked at the Arctic as a place for commerce, a peaceful place, not a militarized part of the world. And what I see today is Russia refurbishing some of its older bases. They are placing in radar, ground forces, et cetera, that could potentially influence the free flow of trade in the Northern Sea Route.

I think our concern is that—they certainly, as you said, you know, that trade route follows most closely to their——

Mr. LARSEN. Right.

General SCAPARROTTI [continuing]. You know, to their border. So they have the right to take steps that most countries would take to secure that.

I think most of our influence is whether they are taking steps that would influence, then, internationally accepted free flow of trade in the North Sea or along the North Sea Route.

Secondly, I am concerned about the high north because their Northern Fleet operates out of there, and they are building capabilities in that, as well, that, just as we did in the Cold War, we have to properly deter and be aware of.

Mr. LARSEN. Yes, that is great. Thank you very much. I yield back.

The CHAIRMAN. Mr. Knight.

Mr. KNIGHT. Thanks, General.

I just have a couple brief questions. I was one of those Grafenwoehr, Reforger, Fulda Gap kind of guys. And looking at the map here, just a quick question to kind of help us understand.

As we were there in the 1980s and there was a totally different aspect of having 50 posts over there and, you know, I don't how many hundred thousand troops were there, compared to today, when NATO is so much different and we have so many more countries that we are working with.

When I was over there with the chairman a couple years ago we were watching Polish soldiers and we were in Romania and it was very enlightening to me to watch the Poles and the Americans work together, and it was just easy to see the symbiotic relationship that they had there.

Tell me how that works. When we are doing three rotations, either a unit is there, a unit is coming home, or a unit is preparing to go. How does that work well when we are talking about Polish soldiers and Romanian, that we can work together and use them for certain areas that we couldn't back in the 1980s, obviously, because of the change to NATO?

General SCAPARROTTI. Well, sir, first thing I think about is the fact that, as you mentioned, our allies in NATO and in Europe, not just—but our partners as well as those 28 nations, you know, they have been overseas with us in Iraq, in Afghanistan, in other areas—Bosnia, Herzegovina, et cetera. Over the years we have developed relationships and we have refined interoperability.

Secondly, we are a force that is used to deploy. I mean, our—all of our military forces, of all services, are good at expeditionary operations and routinely deploying and falling in with host nations, with allies. We have really developed this, and I think that makes a difference. It is what you are talking about.

And so when you see the ease that we work with the Poles, for instance—you mentioned them. I served with the Polish elements in central Iraq; I served with them both tours in Afghanistan. I know many of their leaders. Our forces are used to working together. So when we fall in we know how to communicate, we know how to make those linkages, et cetera.

Mr. KNIGHT. Yes, and I am going to yield back here, Mr. Chairman, but I think that that is one of the most important things to our military right now is our connections to the allies and our connections over the last 20 years or more, even going back to the early 1990s, where we have been in combat with a lot of these folks and we have seen how they react and we have been training with them and they have been training with us. So it is a very close relationship.

Thank you, Mr. Chair.

The CHAIRMAN. Mr. Courtney.

Mr. COURTNEY. Thank you, Mr. Chairman. Thank you, General, for your testimony.

Just want to follow up on Mr. Larsen's questions regarding the high north and the Arctic. I mean, you described, I think very pointedly, the upgrade in terms of military facilities that Russia is engaged in in that part of the world.

There is another aspect, I think, which I wanted to focus on a second, which is that they have actually filed a pretty aggressive claim through UNCLOS [United Nations Convention on the Law of the Sea], in terms of continental shelf rights. And I just wondered if you could sort of talk about that in terms of, again, your concerns about making sure, you know, maritime freedom of the seas continues.

And, of course, as I think you are probably expecting, I just wanted to ask whether you think the U.S. should actually stop handcuffing itself and ratify that treaty so we can get into these kinds of claims—international claims process.

General SCAPARROTTI. Yes, sir. First of all, I don't know the details of their claim, but that is obviously one of the concerns that we have about this for the future. And I do believe that we should be a part of the UNCLOS Treaty.

We adhere to those—to the international norms today already, as most nations do. That simply gives us an actual seat at the table and a vote legally, et cetera.

Mr. COURTNEY. I mean, as we found out with the South China Sea, we actually were not even allowed standing to participate in that ruling——

General SCAPARROTTI. Right.

Mr. COURTNEY [continuing]. Which, again, had just huge consequences in terms of our country's military, you know, posture, et cetera.

So you have also mentioned, you know, again, the focus that you are engaged in in terms of antisubmarine warfare in your opening remarks and a couple other questions.

I guess what I would like to ask is the Office of Naval Intelligence has a document which is unclassified, the Russian Navy Historic Transition, which sort of walks through some of the new shipbuilding activity that Russia is engaged in.

So in terms of, you know, we—you are saying we need to have antisubmarine activity. Why? I mean, what are they doing with submarines?

General SCAPARROTTI. We remain dominant and—you know, as we have been in that arena.

My point is we can't be comforted by that. They are producing several different classes of new submarines. They are very capable and will challenge us, and so we—and we do have plans to increase ours, but we need to continue to invest in that, as well as those other systems that help us with antisubmarine warfare. And I can talk to that in more detail in a closed session, as well.

Mr. COURTNEY. Thank you. Because again, as the—this unclassified document makes clear, I mean, just based on Russia's geography, I mean, the submarine force is the backbone of the Russian navy. It is just where they, you know, where they are situated, that is the platform that can get them out into international waters. Isn't that correct?

General SCAPARROTTI. That is true. The other thing I would point out is the systems that they are placing on them today gives them good reach from wherever they are located, as well. Black Sea, et cetera.

Mr. COURTNEY. Thank you, Mr. Chairman. I yield back.

The CHAIRMAN. Mr. Bacon.

Mr. BACON. Thank you, Mr. Chairman.

And it is an honor to have you here today. Thank you for your leadership and your hard work, and thanks for bringing your J–5/8, one of the smartest guys I know. Good to have him here.

I wanted to just start off by saying I second your desire to put more ground forces in Europe. I think we need it for deterrence. I think it is needed to reassure our Polish and Baltic friends, in particular.

One of the most important missions that you have, in my view, too, is the ballistic missile defense mission that we are doing with Israel right now. Can you give us an update where we are at with that? Are we at a status quo? Are we building onto it? What else do you need for that important mission?

General SCAPARROTTI. Israel, as I said in my comments, is one of our—it is a special ally, but it is one of our closest in Europe. Our staff has very regular and a routine exchange of intelligence and discussions with them. I mean, it is remarkable.

We are just now going through another one of our exercises, and a part of that is the missile defense so that we stay trained as partners in that mission.

That mission is very solid. We continue to train on it; we continue to increase capabilities. The Israelis continue to increase their capabilities, as well.

I do have some needs with respect to that. I am very confident of our ability to support Israel, but I have some needs with respect to that, and I can talk about that in a closed session more specifically.

Mr. BACON. One of the concerns I had—and I was part of that mission early on down at Ramstein—is the mismatch between

Iran's capabilities versus how to defend. And a lot of this defense becomes really deterrence or counterstrike so that they fear, you know, doing the first strike. But that takes a lot of coordination with CENTCOM [U.S. Central Command].

How is that coordination with two different COCOMS [combatant commands] where that seam is right there?

General SCAPARROTTI. An experienced question from having dealt with this seam, but actually, it works very well. We have done integrated planning now any place that we have that the seams, you know, interfere with a plan or be a subject of a plan.

So the dynamic of this environment that we live in, where virtually everything that any one of our COCOMs deals with is multiregional, it has some connection across their border, we have become much more agile at working with each other. I am very confident of our relationship with COCOM, actually, with CENTCOM in particular.

Mr. BACON. One last question. We want to expand our presence in EUCOM, but yet we are still—we are continuing to reduce our infrastructure there. And when I came in in 1985, I think we have cut our presence in Europe by over half, maybe two-thirds even.

And when I was the commander at Ramstein I note that we were continuing to find bases that we wanted to close. Is it prudent to continue to close multiple bases in Europe while we are trying to expand and expand deterrence with Russia?

General SCAPARROTTI. Yes. We have actually taken a look at this since I have been in command; I am sure that General Breedlove did before me.

A good many of those that we had planned for closure I agree with moving on. We have got about 15 left now; there are some of those that we are looking at that I think is worth another look, given the dynamics of the day, because we have got to get our posture right.

So I think holistically, as a program, it was profitable, but there are some of those today that we are going to take a look at that remain.

Mr. BACON. Okay. I appreciate that you are re-looking at that. My instinct tells me we are cutting too much. At the same time realizing that we want to expand, it just doesn't make sense. So thank you.

Chairman, I yield back.

The CHAIRMAN. Ms. Speier.

Ms. SPEIER. Thank you, Mr. Chairman.

General, I have got to tell you, your presentation here is so compelling, and I really appreciate the clarity with which you spelled out the infractions—maybe that is too timid a word to use—but the infractions that Russia has engaged in over these many years. Have you had the opportunity to brief the President?

General SCAPARROTTI. I have not.

Ms. SPEIER. If you were in a position to brief the President and were asked, would you recommend that the President condemn these violations by Russia, in terms of the INF Treaty and the CFE Treaty [Treaty on Conventional Armed Forces in Europe]?

General SCAPARROTTI. Well, I think, you know, first of all, I give best military advice on our military activity, et cetera. That would be a decision that the President would have to make.

Ms. SPEIER. No, I understand that. But do you think that the conduct by Russia rises to the level that would suggest that we speak out publicly about Russia's engagement in so many areas that border Russia?

General SCAPARROTTI. I would say personally that I believe that we should confront the Russians on the violations, et cetera. I have said that publicly, and that would be consistent with my personal opinion or advice.

Ms. SPEIER. Do you think that they have engaged in enough bad behavior that we should impose greater sanctions on them?

General SCAPARROTTI. Again, I think that is something that is considered holistically, but I think that there is—that more, probably, we need to do across the entire government in order to have the proper influence on Russia.

Ms. SPEIER. You have spent a fair amount of time, certainly last week and I believe today as well, when you testified in the Senate about the Russian information warfare campaigns that they have engaged in. And I couldn't agree with you more. I think that we have been asleep at the switch in terms of, you know, showing a countervailing force to their misinformation.

Do you think that in order to kind of beef up our efforts, besides funding Voice of America to a greater degree, what else would you recommend that we do?

General SCAPARROTTI. Well, I think that we have to within our government determine a lead agency that is empowered to integrate the remainder of our government in the information sphere; and then resource, whatever that resourcing level would be, in order to get our message out in a way that is at a level that it has influence.

I just don't think that we are organized to do what we are capable of doing, in terms of the information and the message that we send. And this isn't just about a message to Russia. This is actually about assurance to our allies, et cetera.

Ms. SPEIER. There has been some misinformation, I think, that has been offered up regarding the New START Treaty [Strategic Arms Reduction Treaty] with Russia. Do you think it is a bad deal?

General SCAPARROTTI. As I look back on the treaties and understanding why they were put in place, I think they are actually productive. What we need is to ensure that everyone that is a part of the treaty adheres to the treaty, and then if they don't we decide what steps ought to be taken, as opposed to—in another words, we have to acknowledge whether the treaty is actually in force.

You know, for CFE the Russians have said—I think about 2011 or so they said that they were setting it aside. So these are things that we need to come together and address.

Ms. SPEIER. There was an article in the New York Times, a huge spread, yesterday on, "is our military big enough," and showed, you know, how some of our greatest adversaries, Russia being one, spend $60 billion a year on its military and we spend $540 billion. There was a lot of interesting commentary in that piece about—by persons arguing that, you know, you build up a force when you are going to war.

Do you have any comments about that piece? Did you read it? And if you haven't, I would really be interested in you going through it and giving us some advice on what you agree with and what you don't.

General SCAPARROTTI. All right, thank you. I haven't read it, but I would—I will read it and I will provide you a response if you would like.

Ms. SPEIER. Great. Thank you. I yield back.

[The information referred to was not available at the time of printing.]

The CHAIRMAN. Mr. O'Halleran.

Mr. O'HALLERAN. Thank you, Mr. Chairman. And, General, thank you and your command for all you do for our Nation.

I have a question. I am going to go back to Turkey here for a little bit. You made a statement that Turkey has long been and remains an ally of the United States. That word "remains," why did you put that in there?

General SCAPARROTTI. It just happened to—I put it in there because they remain an ally. To be frank, you know, there is some concern about their drift, given some of the drift to authoritarianism. I would tell you that they remain a close ally with us.

I have spent a good deal of time in Turkey. I have a good relationship with their chief of defense and we are focused on transparency with them, on supporting them in their objectives as well as ours, with respect to countering terrorism and the coalition efforts in Syria. So that is going well, but I do have concern.

Mr. O'HALLERAN. Okay. And your statement also identifies that it—that Turkey maintains a complicated relationship with Russia. Given its position in the Black Sea, and with Syria and Iran and the—its internal conflicts, and everything else that is going on in that area, along with its Russian issues, what is the status of the U.S. military relationship with Turkey, which I think you answered a little bit? What are the challenges moving forward? And what are the implications, given the Russian actions in the region?

General SCAPARROTTI. Again, our mil-to-mil relationship is very good, and despite the attempted coup and the many challenges they face, they have been very committed to both the support of and protection of our forces that operate out of Turkey and are important to our coalition efforts.

Of the challenges that we have, certainly we see all the challenges there that we see in Europe. I mean they have an internal insurgency, a terrorist fight against PKK [Kurdistan Workers' Party]. They have the refugee issue, about 3 million.

And then they have a conflict on their border, where we have troops and are operating as well as Russia, Iran, and others. That is a challenge. And that is part of what we spend a good deal of time on, making sure that we are transparent with each other, we understand each other's objectives and figure out how we can be complementary in that.

But it is probably the most difficult problem set I have seen in my career, frankly.

Mr. O'HALLERAN. And I am sure we can go in further on that, but the—I have sat here and listened to the word "State" or "State Department" mentioned many times and, you know, we have a cut proposed by the President in the State Department budget. What is the importance of the State Department in your role and your ability to complete your mission?

General SCAPARROTTI. Well, the State Department as well as the other agencies are fundamental to what I do in Europe. Again, I strongly believe in a whole-of-government approach. I think that we lead with diplomacy in the State Department, that the military's posture there is to—intent is to give muscle to that diplomacy.

You know, our intent is that we never have to employ our military in a conflict in Europe, that we prevent conflict. And to do that we need a strong diplomatic corps.

Mr. O'HALLERAN. And I guess that is the—just a comment, that is the issue in my head that is problematic as far as any cuts to the State Department, given the other issues that we have in the world and the need for us to maintain strong relationships with all these countries, and especially countries like Turkey, which are so complicated.

And I yield. Thank you, General.

The CHAIRMAN. Mr. Langevin.

Mr. LANGEVIN. Thank you, Mr. Chairman.

General, thank you for your testimony here today and thank you for your great service to our Nation. I regret that I couldn't be here for the early part of the hearing. I was in a competing hearing on—dealing with cybersecurity issues, which is another important topic of national security importance.

But I thank you again for your testimony. So I apologize if some of the things I may have—I may ask have already been covered, but let me get to it.

So, General, I understand that Secretary Tillerson has recently decided to forgo meeting with his NATO counterparts in April and instead travel to Russia later in the month. You know, I wanted to get your perspective on what does this say to our NATO allies that our Secretary of State is choosing to visit with Russia—a nation, by the way, that has meddled in our elections and possibly colluded with the administration—rather than meet with them?

General SCAPARROTTI. Well, as always, you know, when NATO meets, particularly for the foreign ministers conferences, you know, they welcome the United States representative there as one of the central members. It is my understanding now that the meeting will be on the 31st of March and the—NATO agreed with the United States to find a date that was good for all allies.

And so at least my last report, I expect that we will have the foreign ministers on the 31st of March and Secretary Tillerson will be in attendance.

Mr. LANGEVIN. Very good. Thank you for that update.

General SCAPARROTTI. Thank you.

Mr. LANGEVIN. So, General, I know that we just sort of touched on this topic with my colleague who just spoke before I did, but following the President's release of his skinny budget—so I am highly concerned about the potential cuts to the State Department budget, which proposes a 28 percent reduction from last year's levels.

We spend money through the State Department and USAID [U.S. Agency for International Development] in order to further international diplomatic relations so that we might avoid and prevent war. So with a cut like that, what effects do these cuts have in the EUCOM arena, and how will they hinder our allies as we collectively seek to deter an aggressive and unruly Russia?

General SCAPARROTTI. Yes, sir. I can't comment on the cuts themselves or the impact that might have in Europe. State Department will determine that.

But I have said here that the importance of the State Department and the work that we do in European Command is just fundamental.

I have a deputy, for instance, my senior POLAD [Foreign Policy Advisor], is an ambassador and plays a significant role in my headquarters, as do—as does State and all the embassies in all of our missions in Europe. So I think it is paramount that we maintain the capacity to continue to work as a team.

Mr. LANGEVIN. Okay. General, something that is probably often overlooked is that EUCOM is the primary resourcer of personnel and equipment to AFRICOM, which is a growing area of security challenges, if you will. And how does that draw of resources, is that hindering your ability to do your job in the EUCOM arena? And are we not properly resourcing the AFRICOM arena at this point?

General SCAPARROTTI. Yes, sir. The relationship between I and AFRICOM is actually quite good. We do share component commands, and often we deploy forces in support of AFRICOM's operations, so it is working.

It does impact from time to time on my mission as well as General Waldhauser's, because we have a force that is pulled in two different directions at times.

My greatest concern is making sure that we understand risk, I and General Waldhauser, with the Chairman of the Joint Chiefs, that when we deploy forces that haven't been planned for, say a response to a potential crisis or a mission in AFRICOM, that I can verbalize the impact on the EUCOM commission and that we as leaders understand the risk that we are taking in that regard.

That is another way of saying that I think we do need more force structure there. This is working okay. It is a good working relationship. But it does from time to time put a strain on our force and its readiness.

Mr. LANGEVIN. All right. Is your assessment that we are too often taking too much risk in——

General SCAPARROTTI. No, not too often taking too much risk. There have been a couple of times in the year that I have been in command, probably two, that I was concerned enough that I, you know, that we had a discussion and I had a discussion with the Chairman and we—so that we all understood and made the appropriate decision. And so I am confident that we can make the right decision and not take unnecessary risk, but that is—so that gives you an idea of how often that comes up in a year's time.

Mr. LANGEVIN. Thank you, General. I have other questions that I will submit for the record. But I will yield back. Thank you.

The CHAIRMAN. Mr. Lamborn.

Mr. LAMBORN. Thank you, Mr. Chairman.

Thank you, General. And I am going to make this real brief and ask you to answer for the record so that we can keep our schedule moving along here today and also because elements of your answer might be more appropriate in a closed setting.

But I represent Fort Carson, which has an armored brigade combat team over in the Baltics and Bulgaria and Poland. They are doing a great job. They are rotational as opposed to enduring, like you were saying earlier, but I think it has great promise for the future.

But what are the challenges that we are learning from this extended rotation as far as infrastructure and host country capacity and things like that? That is a sensitive topic that I will just take for the record.

And then also, what are our readiness challenges that we are learning and that we need to improve on from a funding standpoint?

I hope to go over and see these great troops later this spring, but if you could supply those answers for the record I would appreciate it.

General SCAPARROTTI. I will. Thank you.

[The information referred to can be found in the Appendix on page 67.]

Mr. LAMBORN. Thank you so much.

The CHAIRMAN. General, we haven't really today touched on your role in dealing with the terrorism threat in Europe. Could you just touch on that briefly?

General SCAPARROTTI. It is one of the central challenges, Chairman, in Europe and with our allies today. In EUCOM we formed a cell as a part of the headquarters that addresses counter—transnational threats to counter those. It is multiagency; it is not just military.

And our concept is a tri-nodal concept of where we are building a relationship with EU, and particularly the Europol, and through the EU nations as well as NATO with a headquarters in JFC [Allied Joint Force Command] Naples, and then with our other partners, as well, outside of NATO, to really strengthen that network.

Everything from information and intelligence sharing, analysis of the transnational threats as, you know, as well as capability—sharing capabilities, building partner capacity, et cetera.

It struck me as I was there that we have, particularly within the alliance, an organization with headquarters, processes, troops if needed, ready-made in order to form a response to this. And all 28 nations in NATO are part of the coalition to fight ISIS today, so I think it fits well and it is one of the key things that we do in Europe.

The CHAIRMAN. And on the 28 nation, did I understand you earlier to say that 22 of the 28 nations are increasing their defense spending this year?

General SCAPARROTTI. That is correct, 22, and 10 within the—there is a 20 percent mandate toward modernization. Ten nations have met that as we go into the year. So that is good news. We expect to see that improving, as well, as we go forward.

The CHAIRMAN. And you have had several questions today about the European Reassurance Initiative and any investments we are making in infrastructure and so forth to make that work. Are the Eastern European nations making investments toward that goal as well?

General SCAPARROTTI. Yes, Chairman, they are. In every country they have invested themselves in facilities to support our mechanized and armored units, in terms of motor pools, et cetera. Barracks facilities, also transportation hubs for the movement of forces.

And so they have also invested. And I think it underscores the importance that they see in our efforts as well as NATO's Enhanced Forward Presence.

The CHAIRMAN. Finally, just a comment. General, today you have gotten a number of questions about Russian violations of the INF Treaty and you have also gotten a number of questions about information warfare, for lack of a better expression.

Both are subjects of some frustration for me. I wrote numerous letters and had numerous briefings on the INF Treaty violations to try to get the Obama administration to take this more seriously, to call the Russians' hands, to have an adequate response. And for some reason they were reluctant to do so.

On information warfare, Mr. Smith and I have been pushing a whole-of-government approach to being more engaged in this ever since the Bush administration, when it became clear that the terrorists were doing a better job than we in information warfare, through the Obama administration.

I am glad to have more people engaged in these issues. We have got some new converts now.

But my point is I want to encourage you to continue to have a strong voice within the military and, because of your—both of your hats, within the government at large. Because for whatever motivation, our government needs to take treaty violations more seriously and to develop better capability on information warfare. I think you can help.

We will certainly be pushing that, as well. And as I say, I am glad to have some new converts to those causes.

With that, this hearing will stand adjourned. And in roughly 5 minutes or so, if it is okay with you, we will get back together upstairs in a classified session.

Thanks.

[Whereupon, at 12:00 p.m., the committee was adjourned.]

APPENDIX

March 28, 2017

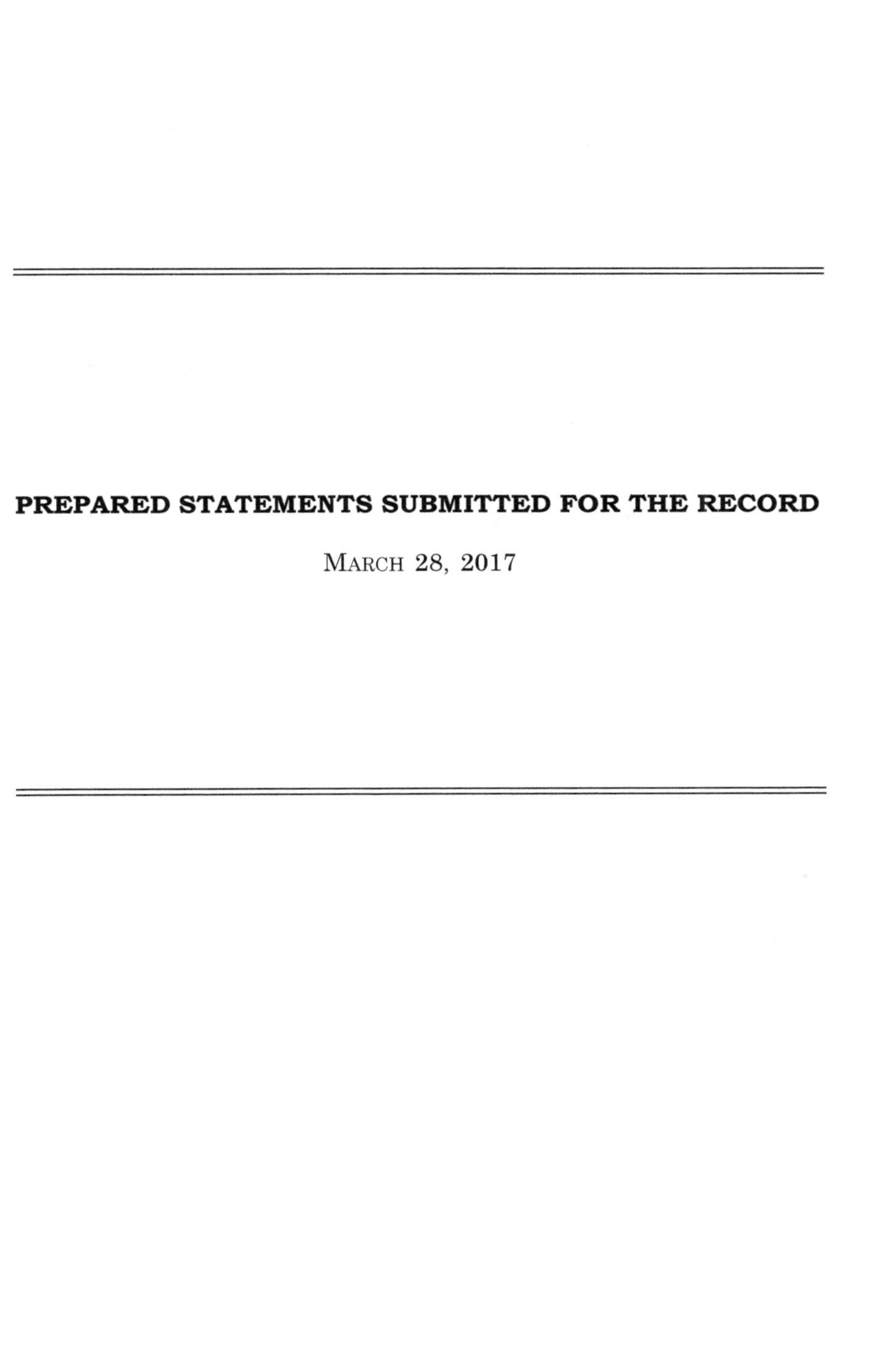

PREPARED STATEMENTS SUBMITTED FOR THE RECORD

MARCH 28, 2017

HOUSE COMMITTEE ON ARMED SERVICES

STATEMENT OF GENERAL CURTIS M. SCAPARROTTI

COMMANDER

UNITED STATES EUROPEAN COMMAND

March 28, 2017

UNCLASSIFIED

I. INTRODUCTION

Mr. Chairman and distinguished members of this Committee, I am honored to testify before you in my first year as the Commander of United States European Command (EUCOM). It is a privilege to lead the great Soldiers, Sailors, Airmen, Marines, Coast Guardsmen, and civilians in this Command. They continue to demonstrate remarkable commitment, dedication, and selfless service both in Europe and across the globe. We all appreciate your continued support.

The European theater remains critical to our national interests. The transatlantic alliance gives us an unmatched advantage over our adversaries--a united, capable, warfighting alliance resolved in its purpose and strengthened by shared values that have been forged in battle. EUCOM's relationship with NATO and the 51 countries within our area of responsibility (AOR) provides the United States with a network of willing partners who support global operations and secure the international rules-based order that our nations have defended together since World War II. Our security architecture protects more than 1 billion people and has safeguarded transatlantic trade, which now constitutes almost half of the world's combined GDP.

Nevertheless, today we face the most dynamic European security environment in history. Political volatility and economic uncertainty are compounded by threats to our security system that are trans-regional, multi-domain, and multi-functional. In the east, a resurgent Russia has turned from partner to antagonist. Countries along Russia's periphery, especially Ukraine and Georgia, are under threat from Moscow's malign influence and military aggression.   In the southeast, strategic drivers of instability converge on key allies, especially Turkey, which has to simultaneously manage Russia,

UNCLASSIFIED

terrorists, and refugee flows. In the south, violent extremists and transnational criminal elements spawn terror and corruption from North Africa to the Middle East, while refugees and migrants fleeing persecution to Europe in search of security and opportunity. In the High North, Russia is reasserting its military prowess and positioning itself for strategic advantage in the Arctic.

EUCOM fully recognizes the dynamic nature of this security environment, and in response, we are regenerating our abilities for deterrence and defense while continuing our security cooperation and engagement mission. This requires that we return to our historical role as a command that is capable of executing the full-spectrum of joint and combined operations in a contested environment. Accordingly, we are adjusting our posture, plans, and readiness to respond to possible future conflicts.

This shift would not be possible without congressional support of the European Reassurance Initiative (ERI). Thanks in large measure to ERI, over the last 12 months EUCOM has made demonstrable progress. U.S. tanks have returned to European soil. U.S. F-15s and F-22s have demonstrated air dominance throughout the theater. U.S. naval forces have sailed throughout European waters. EUCOM has operationalized its Joint Cyber Center. With the approval of former Secretary Carter, EUCOM delivered the first new operational plan for the defense of Europe in over 25 years.

ERI also supports high-end exercises and training, improved infrastructure, and enhanced prepositioning of equipment and supplies, while State Department and DOD funds build partner capacity throughout Europe.

EUCOM has also continued to strengthen our relationship with allies and partners. Our relationship with Turkey endured a coup attempt with minimal disruption

UNCLASSIFIED

to multiple ongoing operations. EUCOM has strengthened ties with Israel, one of our closest allies. Above all, EUCOM has supported the NATO Alliance, which remains, as Secretary Mattis has said, the "bedrock" of our transatlantic security. Overall EUCOM is growing stronger.

II. THEATER ASSESSMENT – RISKS AND CHALLENGES

Over the past year I have highlighted three signature issues facing us in this dynamic security environment: Russia, radicals or violent extremists, and regional unrest – leading to refugee and migrant flows.   At the same time, managing the political, economic, and social challenges posed by refugees and migrants is a consuming concern of our allies and partners.

Russia

Russia's malign actions are supported by its diplomatic, information, economic, and military initiatives. Moscow intends to reemerge as a global power, and views international norms such as the rule of law, democracy, and human rights as components of a system designed to suppress Russia. Therefore, Russia seeks to undermine this international system and discredit those in the West who have created it. For example, Russia is taking steps to influence the internal politics of European countries, just as it tried to do in the United States, in an attempt to create disunity and weakness within Europe and undermine the transatlantic relationship. Furthermore, Russia has repeatedly violated international agreements and treaties that underpin European peace and stability, including the Treaty on Intermediate-Range Nuclear Forces (INF) and the Treaty on Conventional Armed Forces in Europe (CFE), and it is

UNCLASSIFIED

undermining transparency and confidence building regimes, such as the Vienna

Document and Open Skies, which provide greater transparency of posture and exercises

in the region

Russia's political leadership appears to be seeking a resurgence through the

modernization of its military. Russia is adjusting its doctrine, modernizing its weapons,

reorganizing the disposition of its forces, professionalizing its armed services, and

upgrading capabilities in all warfighting domains. Russia desires a military force capable

of achieving its strategic objectives and increasing its power.

Russia's aggression in Ukraine, including occupation and attempted annexation

of Crimea, and actions in Syria underscore its willingness to use military force to exert

its influence in Europe and the Middle East. In Ukraine, Russia's willingness to foment

a bloody conflict into its third year through the use of proxy forces in the Donbas and

elsewhere is deeply troubling to our allies and partners, particularly Russia's closest

neighbors. In Syria, Russia's military intervention has changed the dynamics of the

conflict, bolstered the Bashar al-Assad regime, targeted moderate opposition elements,

compounded human suffering, and complicated U.S. and coalition operations against

the Islamic State of Iraq and Syria (ISIS). Russia has used this chaos to establish a

permanent presence in the Middle East and eastern Mediterranean.

This past year saw other significant demonstrations of Russia's renewed military

capability, including the first ever combat deployment of the KUZNETSOV Task Force,

nation-wide strategic exercises, joint air, ground, and maritime operations in Syria using

new platforms and precision-guided munitions, and the deployment of nuclear-capable

missiles to Kaliningrad. Russia's deployments in Ukraine and Syria also revealed

increased proficiency in expeditionary combat and sustainment operations.

Another key component of Russia's military advancement is its Integrated Air

UNCLASSIFIED

Defense Systems (IADS). For example, in connection with its deployment to support the Assad regime in Syria, Russia fielded advanced Anti-Access / Area Denial (A2/AD) systems that combine command and control, electronic warfare capabilities, and long range coastal defense cruise missiles with advanced air defense platforms. EUCOM assesses that Russia plans to meld existing and future IADS systems into a central command structure to control all air defense forces and weapons.

In the High North, Russia continues to strengthen its military presence through equipment, infrastructure, training, and other activities. Russia is positioning itself to gain strategic advantage if the Northern Sea Route opens and becomes a viable shipping lane between Europe and Asia.

Most concerning, however, is Moscow's substantial inventory of non-strategic nuclear weapons in the EUCOM AOR and its troubling doctrine that calls on the potential use of these weapons to escalate its way out of a failing conflict. Russia's fielding of a conventional/nuclear dual-capable system that is prohibited under the INF Treaty creates a mismatch in escalatory options with the West. In the context of Putin's highly centralized decision-making structure, Moscow's provocative rhetoric and nuclear threats increase the likelihood of misunderstanding and miscalculation.

In addition to recent conventional and nuclear developments, Russia has employed a decades-long strategy of indirect action to coerce, destabilize, and otherwise exercise a malign influence over other nations. In neighboring states, Russia continues to fuel "protracted conflicts." In Moldova, for example, Russia has yet to follow through on its 1999 Istanbul Summit commitments to withdraw an estimated 1,500 troops -- whose presence has no mandate -- from the Moldovan breakaway region of Transnistria. Russia asserts that it will remove its force once a comprehensive settlement to the Transnistrian conflict has been reached.   However, Russia continued

UNCLASSIFIED

to undermine the discussion of a comprehensive settlement to the Transnistrian conflict at the 5+2 negotiations. Moscow continues to play a role in destabilizing the Nagorno-Karabakh dispute by selling arms to both Armenia and Azerbaijan while maintaining troops in Armenia, despite an international pledge to co-chair the Minsk Group, which is charged with seeking resolution of the conflict.

Russia fiercely opposes one of our strongest EUCOM partners, Georgia, in its attempts to align with the European and transatlantic communities. Russia's occupation of Abkhazia and South Ossetia since its 2008 invasion of the Georgian regions has created lasting instability.

In the Balkans, Russia exploits ethnic tensions to slow progress on European and transatlantic integration. In 2016, Russia overtly interfered in the political processes of both Bosnia-Herzegovina and Montenegro.

Additional Russian activities short of war, range from disinformation to manipulation. Examples include Russia's outright denial of involvement in the lead up to Russia's occupation and attempted annexation in Crimea; attempts to influence elections in the United States, France and elsewhere; its aggressive propaganda campaigns targeting ethnic Russian populations among its neighbors; and cyber activities directed against infrastructure in the Baltic nations and Ukraine. In all of these ways and more, Russia is attempting to exert its influence, expand its power, and discredit the capability and relevance of the West.

Radicals

Violent extremists, most notably ISIS, pose a serious, immediate threat to U.S. personnel, our allies, and our infrastructure in Europe and worldwide. In 2016, there were major terrorist attacks in Berlin, Brussels, Istanbul, Nice, Paris, and elsewhere. ISIS has made its intentions clear: it seeks to overthrow Western civilization and

UNCLASSIFIED

establish a world-wide caliphate.

While it's footprint in Iraq and Syria shrunk in 2016, since 2014, ISIS has significantly expanded its operations throughout Europe and now leverages its network to enable and inspire attacks by European-based extremists in their resident countries. Further, ISIS has exploited the migration crisis to infiltrate operatives into Europe. Since Turkey expanded its counter-ISIS role and advocacy for coalition operations in Mosul, it has experienced an increased number of terrorist attacks, and ISIS's leaders have called for more. We do not expect the threat to diminish in the near future.

As a consequence of this threat, European nations have been forced to divert financial resources and military personnel to internal security. The impact of this reallocation is not yet fully appreciated and will likely persist for years. In short, violent extremism poses a dangerous threat to transatlantic nations and to the international order that we value.

Regional Volatility

In EUCOM's AOR, Russia's indirect actions have sought to exploit political unrest and socioeconomic disparities. Russian aggression in Ukraine has led to the deaths of approximately 10,000 people since April 2014. Recently, in eastern Ukraine, Russia has controlled the battle tempo and is again ratcheting up the number of daily violations of the cease fire. Even more concerning, Russia is directing combined Russian-separatist forces to target civilian infrastructure and threaten and intimidate OSCE monitors in order to turn up the pressure on Ukraine. Furthermore, Moscow's support for so-called "separatists" in eastern Ukraine destabilizes Kyiv's political structures just as Ukraine is undertaking politically-difficult reforms to combat corruption and comply with IMF requirements.

Ukraine seeks a permanent and verifiable ceasefire, the withdrawal of heavy

UNCLASSIFIED

weapons and Russian forces, full and unfettered access for OSCE monitors, and control over its internationally-recognized border with Russia. Russian-led separatist forces continue to commit the majority of ceasefire violations despite attempts by the OSCE to broker a lasting ceasefire along the Line of Contact.

Turkey has long been and remains an ally of the United States. It now occupies a critical location at the crossroads of multiple strategic challenges. To its west, it implements the Montreux Convention, which governs transit through the Turkish Straits, and Turkey is committed to local solutions for Black Sea issues. To its north and east, Turkey maintains a complicated relationship with Russia. Ankara seeks to resume the level of trade with Moscow that it enjoyed prior to Turkey's November 2015 shoot down of a Russian fighter. Turkey has absorbed the largest number of refugees from Syria-- almost 3 million. Despite these challenges, EUCOM continues to work closely with Turkey to enable critical basing and logistical support to the counter-ISIS fight and supports Turkey to counter its terror threat.

Although the flow of refugees to Europe has slowed, the refugee situation remains a significant challenge to our European allies and partners. The strain on the social systems of European nations, especially along the Mediterranean Sea, diverts resources that could otherwise go toward military and defense spending, and finding solutions has tested political relationships. EU member states struggle to find a common, "shared" approach to admit and settle migrants. Both NATO and the EU, in conjunction with Turkish and Greek authorities, have committed law enforcement and military assets to this issue, including a maritime force in the Aegean Sea to conduct reconnaissance, monitoring, and surveillance.

The Syrian civil war and the risk of spillover into neighboring states, including Israel, continue to threaten stability in Europe and the Levant. Despite assistance from

UNCLASSIFIED

the USG and the international community, the refugee population in Jordan and

Lebanon has placed significant burdens on the government and local residents.

Additionally, factional fighting in Syria has resulted in occasional cross-border fire into

the Israeli-occupied Golan Heights. Israel has avoided being drawn into the conflict in

Syria but has taken military action to deny the transfer of advanced weapons to

Hezbollah.

The Balkans' stability since the late 1990's masks political and socio-economic

fragility. Russia promotes anti-European views in this region by exploiting corrupt

political systems, poor economic performance, and increased ethnic polarization.

Additionally, Islamic radicals seek to take advantage of high unemployment rates,

political turmoil, and socioeconomic disparities to recruit violent extremists.

Iran's regional influence in the Levant continues to grow through its ongoing

support to radical groups such as Lebanese Hezbollah, Hamas, Palestinian Islamic

Jihad, and paramilitary groups involved in the Syrian conflict and in counter-ISIS efforts

across Iraq. Iran, which Israel views as its greatest existential threat, continues to

transfer advanced conventional arms to Hezbollah and is clearly committed to

maintaining Syria as the key link of the Iran-Hezbollah axis, which sustains a terrorist

network in Syrian-regime controlled territory. Furthermore, Iran has taken advantage of

the Syrian crisis to militarily coordinate with Russia in support of Assad.

III. THEATER ASSESSMENT - STRENGTHS AND OPPORTUNITIES

EUCOM will meet these challenges and adapt to the new security environment

by capitalizing on our strengths and building new capabilities. We are developing a

credible and relevant force structure built for deterrence and defense, leveraging a

unified and adaptive NATO Alliance, and transitioning into a command able to address

UNCLASSIFIED

the strategic challenges before us.

Deter Russia

EUCOM activities, facilitated by ERI funding, continue to be the primary demonstration of our deterrent capability.

Increased Rotational Forces. ERI has directly supported an increase in the rotational presence of U.S. forces in Europe, a critical augmentation to EUCOM's assigned forces. For example, ERI funded Fort Stewart's 1st Armored Brigade Combat Team's deployment to Europe from March to September 2016. Also, ERI funded the deployment of F-22 fighters, B-52 bombers, and additional combat and lift aircraft to Europe as part of the ERI Theater Security Package. Looking ahead, continued congressional support for ERI will sustain these rotations and enable additional anti-submarine warfare capabilities, complementing maritime domain awareness assets in Iceland that are included in the FY 2017 ERI request. Additionally, rotational Marine units will operate from Norway and the Black Sea region.

Trained and Equipped Component Commands. EUCOM has also used ERI to fund and field Army Prepositioned Stocks (APS), providing a rapid mobilization capability for additional armored units in Europe. Separately, EUCOM advocated for and received full support for a $220 million NATO Security Investment Program project (i.e., paid for by NATO common funding) that will build warehousing and maintenance capability for staging APS stocks in Poland. Additionally, ERI funds dozens of projects to upgrade flight-line and munitions-storage infrastructure across eight NATO nations to support not only rotational presence but also training events in Eastern Europe. The Navy is using ERI to fund capability enablers and force rotations to support EUCOM and NATO exercises, including mine countermeasures teams and additional flying hours, specifically to enhance EUCOM's deterrence posture.

UNCLASSIFIED

<u>Persistent Presence</u>. ERI increased funding for U.S. forces in the Baltics, Poland, Romania, Bulgaria, and the Mediterranean during 2016. In addition, ERI allowed EUCOM to continue our contribution to NATO's Air Policing mission by funding a continued fighter presence in theater with the 493rd Fighter Squadron at RAF Lakenheath in the UK.

<u>Complex Exercises with Allies and Partners</u>. ERI expanded the scope of EUCOM's involvement in over 28 joint and multi-national maritime, air, amphibious, and ground exercises across 40 countries. In June 2016, EUCOM participated in the Polish national exercise ANAKONDA, which involved approximately 31,000 Allied troops, including over 14,000 U.S. personnel, and provided a robust demonstration of Allied defensive capabilities, readiness, and interoperability. ERI also supported Navy-led BALTOPS 16, the premier maritime exercise in the Baltic region with over 6,100 troops from participating nations. And utilizing ERI resources, the Air Force took part in over 50 exercises and training deployments across Europe. An Acquisition and Cross-Servicing Agreement concluded with the EU last December enables EUCOM to cooperate better with EU missions in the Balkans and elsewhere.

<u>Russia Strategic Initiative (RSI)</u>: EUCOM leads the Department of Defense's Russia Strategic Initiative (RSI), which provides a framework for understanding the Russian threat and a forum for coordinating efforts and requirements. RSI allows us to maximize the deterrent value of our activities while avoiding inadvertent escalation. In just over a year, RSI has created a number of analytic products for combatant commanders that will enable a more efficient application of existing resources and planning efforts.

Deterring Russia requires a whole of government approach, and EUCOM supports the strategy of approaching Russia from a position of strength while seeking

UNCLASSIFIED

appropriate military-to-military communication necessary to fulfill our defense obligations in accordance with the National Defense Authorization Act for Fiscal Year 2017. Going forward, we must bring the information aspects of our national power more fully to bear on Russia, both to amplify our narrative and to draw attention to Russia's manipulative, coercive, and malign activities. Finally, NATO and U.S. nuclear forces continue to be a vital component of our deterrence. Our modernization efforts are crucial; we must preserve a ready, credible, and safe nuclear capability.

Enable the NATO Alliance

As the United States manages multiple strategic challenges, our enduring strength remains NATO, the most successful alliance in history. NATO's leadership understands that the security environment has radically changed over the past few years. The Alliance has placed renewed emphasis on deterring further Russian aggression, countering transnational threats, such as violent extremist organizations, and projecting stability in the Middle East and North Africa, while fulfilling its commitments in Afghanistan.

The Warsaw Summit last July was a significant demonstration of unity, cooperation, and strategic adaptation. As the member nations declared in NATO's Warsaw Summit Communiqué, "We are united in our commitment to the Washington Treaty, the purposes and principles of the Charter of the United Nations (UN), and the vital transatlantic bond." This unity is NATO's center of gravity, and the United States must continue to support solidarity among the Alliance nations.

Enhanced Forward Presence (eFP). The signature outcome of the 2016 Warsaw Summit was the decision to establish an enhanced Forward Presence (eFP) in the Baltics and Poland to demonstrate NATO's cohesion in defense of the Alliance. Canada, Germany, the United Kingdom, and the United States have begun deploying

UNCLASSIFIED

multinational battalion task forces to Latvia, Lithuania, Estonia, and Poland, respectively, on a rotational basis. Defense Cooperation Agreements (DCAs) signed in 2017 with Estonia, Latvia, and Lithuania are facilitating the deployment of U.S forces there. The United States serves as the framework nation for eFP in Poland and is working closely with the other framework nations and their host nations to ensure NATO's key deterrence and defense measures are capable and integrated.

European Phased Adapted Approach (EPAA). EUCOM continues to implement the EPAA to defend European NATO populations, territory, and infrastructure against ballistic missile threats from outside the Euro-Atlantic region. In July 2016, the U.S.-funded Aegis Ashore facility in Romania became operational and transferred to NATO operational control. Work on the Aegis Ashore site in Poland (authorized and appropriated in fiscal year 2016 legislation) is underway and on track for completion by the end of calendar year 2018 and operational under NATO operational control in mid-2019.

Projecting Stability. NATO is a key contributor to ensuring security and projecting stability abroad. It is worth remembering that the first and only time the Alliance invoked the mutual defense provisions of its founding treaty was in response to the 9/11 attacks on the United States. Today, through NATO's Resolute Support Mission, over 12,000 troops (including over 5,000 non-U.S. personnel) provide training and assistance to Afghan security forces and institutions. NATO is committed to ensuring a stable Afghanistan that is not a safe haven for terrorists.

Additionally, it is notable that all 28 NATO nations participate in the counter-ISIS coalition. NATO committed AWACS surveillance aircraft and actively contributes to capacity building in Iraq. EUCOM supports NATO's goal of expanding its operations against this terrorist threat.

UNCLASSIFIED

<u>Support to Washington Treaty</u>. EUCOM provides support for key articles of the Washington Treaty, enabling NATO members to meet their collective security commitments. EUCOM conducts activities, such as security cooperation, to help allies meet their Article 3 commitment to "maintain and develop their individual and collective capacity to resist attack." We have been able to reduce allies' dependencies on Russian-sourced, legacy military equipment thanks to ongoing congressional support for critical authorities and funding that provide shared resources. EUCOM also actively assists the Alliance when an ally declares, under Article 4, that its territorial integrity, political independence, or security is threatened. The last time an ally invoked Article 4 was 2015 when Turkey sought consultation following terrorist attacks. Most importantly, EUCOM is the force that backs the United States commitment to Article 5, which declares that an armed attack on one ally is an attack on all.

<u>NATO Spending Trends</u>. At the Wales Summit in 2014, the allies pledged to reverse the trend of declining defense budgets and invest in the development of highly-capable and deployable forces. Today, in addition to the United States, four allies (Estonia, Greece, Poland, and the United Kingdom) meet the NATO guidelines for 2% of GDP, up from three in 2014. Allies' defense expenditures increased in 2015 for the first time since 2009 and grew at a real rate of 3.8% in 2016, with 22 member nations increasing defense spending. Allies are showing demonstrable progress toward their commitment to contribute 2% of their GDP by 2024.

This is a positive trend, but allied nations must meet the 2% mark with 20% allocated to the modernization of equipment and infrastructure. Critical ally and partner capability shortfalls remain, including strategic lift; intelligence, surveillance, and reconnaissance (ISR); deployable command and control; air to air refueling; and air and missile defense. Further, both EUCOM and NATO are hampered by inadequate

UNCLASSIFIED

infrastructure that affects the ability to maneuver across the continent. The expansion of the Alliance to include former Eastern Bloc countries has exacerbated the lack of common transportation networks between the newer NATO members in the east and the more established allies in the west. EUCOM is working closely with NATO to identify and address infrastructure requirements to improve U.S. and NATO freedom of movement throughout the theater.

Build Partner Capacity

EUCOM has spent several decades working with the Department of State to help allied and partner nations develop and improve their military and other security forces. This partner capacity building has been accomplished with the support of this Committee, which has been generous in providing us the authorization we need to accomplish this critical task. I would highlight two activities in particular.

Defense Institution Building (DIB). DIB helps partner nations build effective, transparent, and accountable defense institutions. For example, EUCOM fully endorses the work of the Defense Reform Advisory Board in Ukraine, which is helping to bring about both political and military reform as the Ministry of Defense, General Staff, and Armed Forces transition from centralized Soviet-style systems and concepts towards a Euro-Atlantic model. We also support defense institutions in Georgia, helping them improve their strategic logistics, human and material resource management, and institutional aspects of their training management system. Overall, our DIB efforts lay the groundwork for broader security cooperation activities.

Joint Multinational Training Group Ukraine (JMTG-U). Together with forces from Lithuania, Latvia, Estonia, the UK, and Canada, using State Department-provided Foreign Military Financing and Ukraine Security Assistance Initiative funds, EUCOM trains, advises, and equips Ukraine security forces, helping them build the capacity to

UNCLASSIFIED

defend their sovereignty and territorial integrity. Our team, working through the

Multinational Joint Commission, has developed Ukraine's institutional training capability

so that Ukraine can create a NATO-interoperable armed force. Our efforts include the

training of both conventional and special operations units, as well as advising Ukraine

on defense reform priorities.

Assist Israel

EUCOM's mission to assist in the defense of Israel, one of our closest allies,

remains a top priority. Success will depend on the continued support of Congress and

our strong relationship with the Israel Defense Forces. Many aspects of our bilateral

relationship have been guided by the Strategic Cooperation Initiative Program (SCIP)

framework, which dates to the Reagan administration. SCIP enables robust

cooperation and coordination on a vast range of security matters. Going forward, we

are working to update the SCIP to incorporate an examination of all major exercises to

ensure each meets the three major pillars of our security relationship: (1) missile

defense, air operations, and counter-terrorism; (2) managing the Weapon Reserve

Stockpile for Allies-Israel (WRSA-I); and (3) ensuring Israel's qualitative military edge.

Counter Transnational Threats

Adopting a whole-of-government approach, EUCOM, together with its

interagency partners, conducts initiatives to counter transnational threats including

countering terrorism and the flow of foreign fighters, countering illicit finance networks,

combatting the trafficking of persons and illicit substances, and building allied and

partner security, investigative, and judicial capacity. In conjunction with the

Departments of State, Justice, Homeland Security, and other federal law enforcement

agencies, EUCOM works to monitor and thwart the flow of foreign fighters, support the

dismantlement of facilitation networks, and build partner nation capacity to defeat violent

UNCLASSIFIED

extremism.

Through our counterterrorism cell, EUCOM strengthens global counter-ISIS efforts in coordination with and support of U.S. Central (CENTCOM), Africa (AFRICOM), and Special Operations (SOCOM) Commands. We have focused on those who facilitate the ISIS brand and network through radicalization, financing, and propaganda.

Also, EUCOM and NATO are working to increase ties with the EU to enhance the capabilities Europe can collectively bring to bear against transnational threats. These three organizational nodes foster a shared understanding of the threats, help match resources accordingly, and can address all elements of national power including diplomatic, informational, military, and economic. In order to realize this networked approach, EUCOM will support NATO efforts to expand the capability and capacity of Allied Joint Forces Command – Naples.

Enable Global Operations

EUCOM personnel actively support operations in AFRICOM and CENTCOM AORs. EUCOM's well-developed and tested infrastructure provides critical capabilities in strategic locations such as Incirlik, Turkey; Sigonella, Italy; and Morón and Rota, Spain. Basing and access in Germany, Greece, Italy, France, Spain, Turkey, and the United Kingdom enable more timely and coordinated trans-regional crisis response.

IV. RESOURCE REQUIREMENTS

Significant U.S. force reductions following the collapse of the Soviet Union were based on the assumption that Russia would be a strategic partner to the West. These reductions now limit U.S. options for addressing challenges in a changing European strategic environment. The strategic rebalance to Asia and the Pacific, combined with budget limitations in the Budget Control Act of 2011, have contributed to substantial

UNCLASSIFIED

posture reductions across our land and air domains. For example, between 2010 and 2013, two fighter squadrons and a two-star numbered air force headquarters were inactivated, along with associated critical enablers and staff personnel. In addition, the last two heavy Brigade Combat Teams (BCT), a two-star division headquarters, and a three-star corps headquarters were removed from Europe, leaving only one Stryker and one airborne brigade. As a result of the BCT losses, without fully-resourced heel-to-toe rotational forces, the ground force permanently assigned to EUCOM is inadequate to meet the combatant command's directed mission to deter Russia from further aggression.

Deterrence Posture. Going forward, we will need to continue maintaining capable forces for effective deterrence. EUCOM is coordinating across the DoD to obtain the forces we need in every warfare domain. This may include additional maneuver forces, combat air squadrons, anti-submarine capabilities, a carrier strike group, and maritime amphibious capabilities. We will continue to enhance our plans for pre-positioning equipment across the theater as a flexible deterrent measure and to exercise the joint reception, staging, and onward integration of CONUS-based forces into Europe.

ERI Requirements. EUCOM continues to require the ability to deter Russian aggression and counter malign influence while assuring allies and partners. We anticipate needing to continue deterrence measures initiated in previous ERI submissions, to include Army and Air Force prepositioning, retention of F-15 presence, improved airfield infrastructure improvements, and to address some new capabilities needed in the theater.

Indications and Warnings (I&W). EUCOM's ability to provide strategic warning is critical to credible deterrence. A robust intelligence capability enables accurate analysis

UNCLASSIFIED

and rapid response in a changing theater security environment. This capability also

supports the design of realistic exercises, posture alignment, and future requirements.

Furthermore, when completed, EUCOM's Joint Intelligence Analytic Center at Royal Air

Force Croughton will provide a dedicated, purpose-built intelligence facility collocated

with NATO and AFRICOM's analytic centers that will enhance capability and capacity in

both combatant commands and NATO. Finally, additional intelligence collection

platforms in theater, such as the U-2, the RQ-4, and the RC-135, are required for

accurate and timely threat information to support strategic decisions.

Recapitalization Efforts. The European Infrastructure Consolidation effort

announced in January 2015 enables EUCOM to divest excess capacity and consolidate

missions and footprints at enduring locations. However, with aging infrastructure and

little recent investment, recapitalization and consolidation projects are required to

support warfighter readiness, command and control requirements, deployments,

training, and quality of life. This Committee has been key to these critical efforts. We

continue to modernize communications facilities and schools across Europe. Last year,

Congress authorized the final increment for the Joint Intelligence Analysis Center, which

enables the closure of RAFs Molesworth and Alconbury.

V. CONCLUSION

Let me conclude by again thanking this Committee's Members and staff for their

continued support of EUCOM, not only by providing our requested funding, but also by

helping us to articulate the challenges that lie before us. Support from other senior

leaders and, above all, from the public at home and across Europe is vital to ensuring

that we remain ready and relevant. This is a pivotal time for EUCOM as we transition

to meet the demands of a dynamic security environment. I remain confident that

UNCLASSIFIED

through the strength of our Alliance and partnerships, and with the professionalism of

our service members, we will adapt and ensure that Europe remains whole, free and at

peace.

General Curtis M. Scaparrotti
Commander, U.S. European Command and
NATO Supreme Allied Commander Europe

U.S. Army Gen. Curtis M. Scaparrotti assumed duties as Commander of European Command and as Supreme Allied Commander, Europe in late spring of 2016.

General Curtis M. Scaparrotti is a native of Logan, Ohio, graduated from the United States Military Academy, West Point, in 1978, and was commissioned as a Second Lieutenant in the U.S. Army.

A career infantry officer, General Scaparrotti was previously assigned as the Commander, United Nations Command / Combined Forces Command / United States Forces Korea. He also served as the Director, Joint Staff. Prior to his tour with the Joint Staff, General Scaparrotti served as Commander, International Security Assistance Force Joint Command and Deputy Commander, U.S. Forces–Afghanistan, the Commanding General of I Corps and Joint Base Lewis-McChord, and the Commanding General of the 82nd Airborne Division.

In addition, General Scaparrotti has served in key leadership positions at the tactical, operational, and strategic level of the United States military to include Director of Operations, United States Central Command and as the 69th Commandant of Cadets at the United States Military Academy. He has commanded forces during Operations IRAQI FREEDOM, ENDURING FREEDOM (Afghanistan), SUPPORT HOPE (Zaire/Rwanda), JOINT ENDEAVOR (Bosnia-Herzegovina), and ASSURED RESPONSE (Liberia).

His military education includes the Infantry Officer Basic and Advanced Courses, Command and General Staff College, and the United States Army War College. He holds a Master's Degree in Administrative Education from the University of South Carolina.

His awards and decorations include the Defense Distinguished Service Medal, Distinguished Service Medal, Defense Superior Service Medal, Legion of Merit, Bronze Star, and the Army Meritorious Service Medal. He has earned the Combat Action Badge, Expert Infantryman Badge, Master Parachutist Badge, and Ranger Tab.

WITNESS RESPONSES TO QUESTIONS ASKED DURING THE HEARING

MARCH 28, 2017

RESPONSE TO QUESTION SUBMITTED BY MR. LAMBORN

General SCAPARROTTI. As the first of continuous "heel-to-toe" rotations of heavy brigades to deploy a full armor equipment set and personnel from the United States to Europe, we are continuously learning specific infrastructure challenges. We are testing logistical networks, transportation routes, host nation capacity, infrastructure, and the supporting capabilities of the NATO Force Integration Units through a series of multi-national exercises and the simultaneous rotation of the inbound 2/1 rABCT and outbound 3/4 rABCT in September 2017. So far we have validated transportation issues such as limited access to rail and the low availability of EU compliant trucks and trailers. ERI investments from FY15–FY17 funded upgrades to several rail heads, vehicle maintenance facilities and training areas with several projects already complete or currently underway. ERI also funded improvements at several airfields that will enable the deployment and positioning of combat and mobility airpower. With our NATO partners, we continue to focus on rapid mobility, capturing lessons learned, and identifying gaps at airfields, seaports, rail, transportation, storage and distribution centers, and life support areas. Finally, ERI is also funding meaningful exercises for the rABCT that facilitates extensive exercising with Allies which maintains the brigade's readiness at a high level. [See page 36.]

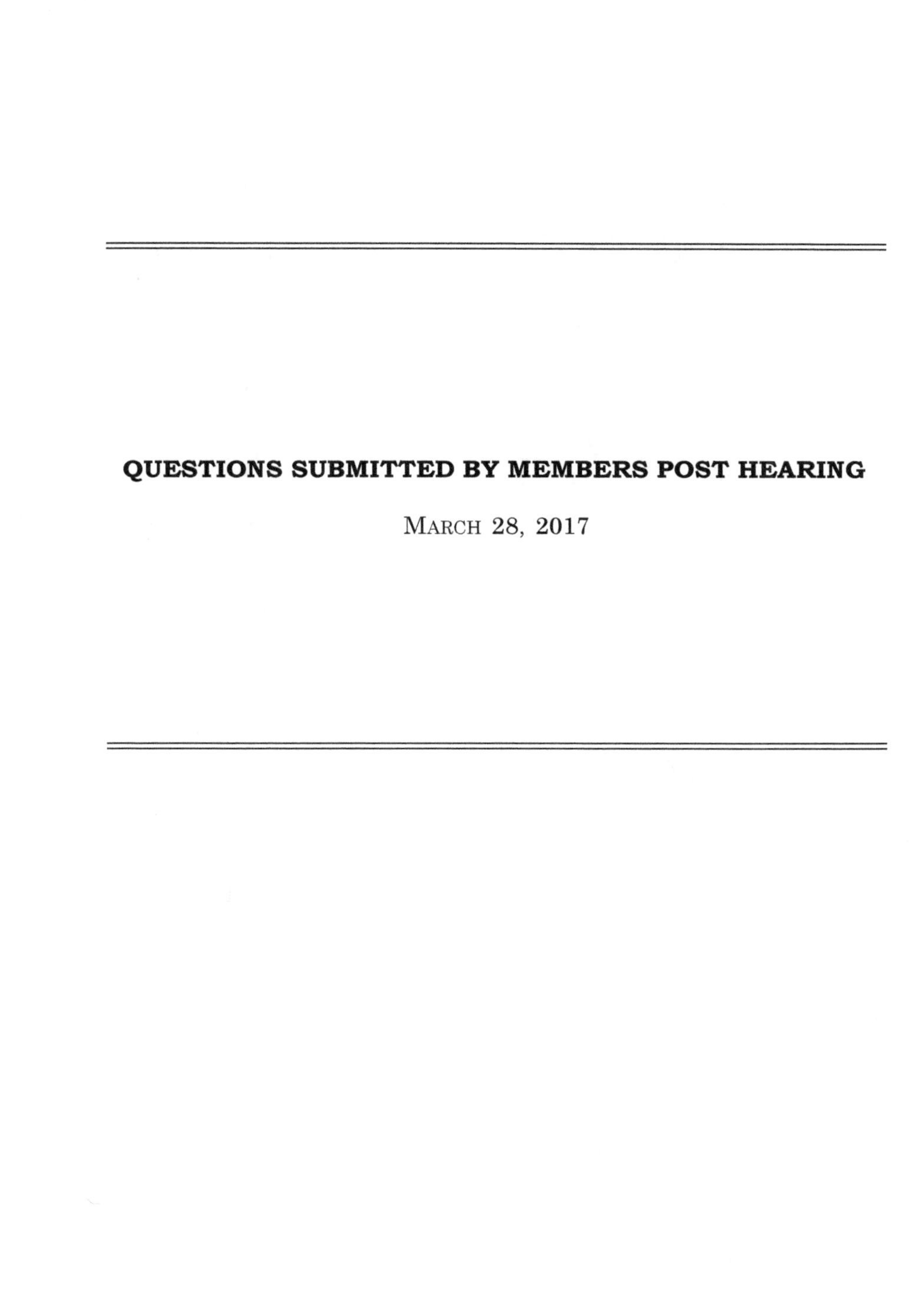QUESTIONS SUBMITTED BY MEMBERS POST HEARING

MARCH 28, 2017

QUESTIONS SUBMITTED BY MR. SCOTT

Mr. SCOTT. The E–8C Joint Surveillance Target Attack Radar System (JSTARS) plays a critical national security role supporting combatant commands around the globe. In your previous position as Commander of U.S. Forces Korea you had personal experience with the weapon system and expressed its value in your Korean theater. With its ability to sweep large areas with its wide area surveillance radar and ability to provide responsive on-scene command and control with its battle management crew, it detects potential adversary movements and vectors other scarce ISR or strike platforms directly to a potential target, increasing their effectiveness exponentially. The Air Force is currently pursuing a recapitalization of the JSTARS to replace the aging fleet. With the growing threats in your theater, and experience employing the JSTARS in another part of the world, would you please characterize the contribution the JSTARS would bring to your current warfighting mission? Realizing there is currently insufficient JSTARS capacity to meet combatant command requirements, are you concerned there may be an increased gap in capacity if we remove current capability from the force structure prior to transitioning to the recapitalized system?

General SCAPARROTTI. As our strategy and military activities evolve from engagement and assurance to deterrence and defense, the surveillance capability provided by JSTARS and similar platforms become more important. This capability provides needed Indications and Warning of Russian troop movements along NATO's eastern border and is key to our readiness to counter Russia. As with all high demand, low density Airborne ISR capabilities, requirements far outstrip capacity, therefore any decreases in ISR assets would increase the delta between requirements and ability for those requirements to be satisfied.

QUESTIONS SUBMITTED BY MR. MOULTON

Mr. MOULTON. European Reassurance Initiative (ERI) has been an important policy to provide support to our allies and counter Russia. However, I am concerned that deployments of ground troops, aircraft squadrons—while critically necessary—are not sufficient in themselves to counter Russia's insidious hybrid warfare. How can we better tailor ERI to address this? Particularly, covert influence and information warfare—how can we provide additional or new legislative authority or budgetary resources to ensure these methods of Russian influence are countered?

General SCAPARROTTI. The Information Operations program is one of the EUCOM commander's most powerful tools to challenge an adversaries disinformation and propaganda, expose the false narratives that accompany "hybrid warfare," counter violent extremist messaging, and share the information environment prior to and during a crisis. We currently do not need any new legislative authorities and are working Information Operations requirement through our established ERI process to ensure we use these funds in the best areas to get the desired result. The best way to counter this type of warfare is thru a whole of government approach. We are actively participating in the interagency, State Department led, Russia Information Group (RIG) which is looking at new ways to counter Russia's massive hybrid warfare campaign. Outcomes from this interagency working group may result in the need for new authorities or budget resources.

QUESTIONS SUBMITTED BY DR. ABRAHAM

Dr. ABRAHAM. With last year's coup attempt in Turkey and the potential for political instability ahead of this year's April presidential referendum there, what are some of the challenges you have faced and expect to face with U.S. and coalition basing access to Incirlik Air Base? Have we faced similar access issues with other allies who experienced political instability in the past?

General SCAPARROTTI. Last year's coup attempt in Turkey created several initial challenges for EUCOM. These included cutting power and fuel supplies to Incirlik AB that were all quickly resolved. Presently, we do not expect the Turkish political situation will play a persistent role with regards to Allied access at Incirlik AB. For the purposes of flexibility, we have assessed alternative basing options, not only for Incirlik AB but throughout the EUCOM AOR. While EUCOM is prepared to shift our assets from Incirlik if required, we are working closely with Turkish military and political leadership to ensure a long, continued basing and access relationship with our Turkish Ally. Access challenges are not limited to Turkey, and we have been required to work through freedom of movement and access issues with forward based troops in many of our Allies throughout the years.

www.ingramcontent.com/pod-product-compliance
Lightning Source LLC
Chambersburg PA
CBHW081317250726
48662CB00008B/2622